Identity: The Key to Fast Track Your Career Success

The 5-Step Blueprint to Discovering Your Identity, Greater Self Love, Passion, Happiness and Success

Trish Mackenzie

Identity: The Key to Fast Track Your Career Success

© **Trish Mackenzie 2012**

A CreateSpace Paperback

Printed in The United States by CreateSpace
First published in 2012.

All rights reserved. No part of this publication may be reproduced, stored in a retrieval system, or transmitted, in any form or by any means, internet, electronic, mechanical, photocopying, recording or otherwise, without the expressed permission of the owner.

ISBN: 978-0-646-58735-6

Editor: Ingrid Carson
Formatting : Print-tech
Cover Design: Lavilamedia
Illustrations: Wealth Dynamics Profiling System, Kobe A Index,
EFT Tapping Diagram, The Gamut Point

National Library of Australia
Cataloguing-in-Publication Data:

Trish Mackenzie
Identity: The Key to Fast Track Your Career Success

ISBN: 978-0-646-58735-6
1. Personal Development
2. Self Help

I Dedicate This Book To

The loving memory of my mother, Monica Lelacheur, who passed away in late 2009.

Thank you for always believing in my talents and being the catalyst for my life altering move to The Southern Highlands of NSW, Australia.

The most wonderful group of supportive and nurturing people of Bowral and surrounds —my neighbours, new friends, work colleagues, church group and the amazing townsfolk.

I extend my heartfelt gratitude to you for helping me heal and find my way back to love.

Blessings.

About the Author

Trish Mackenzie found her identity, her true spiritual, and human Life Path and Purpose, by using the techniques described in this, her first book. With professional qualifications in accounting, mass communications, education and counseling, Trish has done everything from tutoring and lecturing in accounting, to running an accounting practice, making a movie, to mentoring girls and women in business, to opera singing.

She wrote, directed and produced her first short film, *The Rip-Off*, and, as a hobby, is dabbling in the process of developing her other movie scripts. As head of her own accounting practice, Trish was a finalist in the Telstra Women in Business Awards. As a counselor, Trish was a finalist in the Sydney Business Review Weekly Women in Business Awards. She gave up her accounting practice to follow her true identity, and follow her Life Path as an inspirational writer, counselor and speaker.

Having clarified her identity, knowing her unique natural talents and spiritual role on the planet, and being able to fully express her highest values in the 'vehicle' that is right for her, Trish is now well on the way to the success she deserves.

Trish lives in Bowral, New South Wales, Australia with her two cats, Princess and Leo, where she practices as a Life Path Counsellor and Coach to individuals and businesses. Information about Trish's books, seminars, webinars and e-courses are available on her website. www.learntobesuccessfulnow.com.

Foreword

Wow! In this inspiring, easy-to-follow book, *Identity: The Key to Fast Track Your Career Success*, Trish Mackenzie captures the essence of how to live a rich and meaningful life, on track, and on the right path to success. Hers is a no-nonsense approach to finding your identity, your true Life Path and getting on the fast track to success in your career, and your life in general, to finding greater self love, greater passion, happiness and inevitably greater success, not only in your career, but in life in general, living the life you deserve, NOW—not some distant time in the future.

Using real examples from her own life, Trish bravely identifies the obstacles and frustrations so many people encounter trying to find their place in the world. I love the way Trish uses the experience of making her movie, *The Rip-Off*, as the concrete framework to show how the five steps all fit together. She also incorporates practical daily tools and techniques that will help you get your goals in focus and achieve them effortlessly. *Identity: The Key to Fast Track Your Career Success* cuts to the heart of the matter, giving you a clear blueprint for finding the direction you need—and FAST!

As an Innovator, Trish uses her natural talents to bring together some of the best ideas in the self-development world. She clearly demonstrates how the Wealth Dynamics profiling system can work together with the Kolbe A Index to give you profound insight into your natural talents base. At this level, you experience a deep sense of validation, and that's a powerful place to come from. Having this knowledge will put you on the path of least resistance—and hence, your best and most effortless path—to knowing your identity, and to attracting both inner and outer wealth.

The most remarkable thing about Trish's book is the unique way she has collated so many different ideas into one cohesive whole—delivering you, the reader, the complete toolbox for success in your career. Once you have discovered your Life Path and natural talents base, Trish shows you how to use this information to your best advantage. She offers concrete, real-world tips on how to set the goals that are most appropriate to you, and outlines the goal setting strategies from my bestselling book, *Double Your Income Doing What You Love*.

If you want to fast track your progress towards your career success, greater self love, passion, happiness, and overall success in life, Trish shows you how, from beginning to end. With her daily tools and techniques, you'll be able to stay focused and clear away any negativity that detracts from your attractiveness factor. From establishing a foundation, to discovering your true talents and setting goals, to maintaining a daily state of joy and abundance—*Identity: The Key to Fast Track Your Career Success* has what you need, to turbo-charge your path to your career success.

I highly recommend this book to anyone who wants to experience real wealth, both inner and outer, by discovering their unique identity. If you are ready to live the life you deserve, now!—don't hesitate to read this book. You'll be inspired to become the person that you know is inside you—your best and happiest self. Armed with knowledge of your own unique identity, will give you your personal blueprint for success in your career. Who knows? Maybe we will even hear about your success firsthand once you've taken the up the challenge of *Identity: The Key to Fast Track Your Career Success*.

Love
Raymond Aaron
New York Times Top Ten Bestselling Author
www.OwnTheEdge.com

Preface

This edition of my book, *Identity: The Key to Fast Track Your Career Success,* has been re-released with more of a focus on how to fast track your career success. This will help you answer the question: Who am I? Where do I fit in? What is my identity?

This book is specifically designed for those of you who need a new career direction but do not know where to start. I will show you how to take definite steps towards the career success that is rightfully yours. There really is a way to make sure you're doing what you love in your job, career or business. The key is clarifying the individual elements that make up your own unique *identity*.

In my first edition of this book, I talk about a spiritual Life Path perspective. From this perspective, we see that, fundamentally, our inner essence, our real self, and our real purpose in life—is one of love. We need to love ourselves before we can truly love another. Often, in order to move forward in life, we have to make difficult decisions and sometimes take what looks like the hard road.

But the miracle of the "hard road" is that truly it is the path of least resistance! It just may not appear that way at first, because we have to let go of bad habits and stop procrastinating. You see, lack of love shows up when we continue to do what we are already doing and expect a different result. So often in life, we become scared of making a change so we just keep going to the same unsatisfying job, doing the same unsatisfying thing over and over, because we can't commit to taking those first steps. If we want to change our lives significantly, we need to start taking baby steps, doing something every day towards that end.

This book is your blueprint for those baby steps, and for putting your life back on the fast track to success. From a practical point of view, if you are frustrated, stressed-out and looking for more meaning in your working life, you need solutions to your most pressing problems. You need information. You need clear guidance and direction. If there is any short-cut to career success, you need to know about it *now*. This is what this book is about. It is about finding a clear path to success, particularly in your working life. It is about defining who you are.

The most common problem for people struggling with great unrest in their job, career or business life is that they really *do not know who they are*. They don't exactly know how they arrived in the position they occupy. They are not aware of the innate, natural skills and talents that make up the unique individual they are. In other words, they do not know their identity. This book aims to address this problem and come up with a workable solution: the five-step blueprint.

This edition details a five-step blueprint to uncovering your identity. It starts at the spiritual level and moves through practical steps to clarify the Life Path that is right for you. We look at innate skills and abilities, the natural talents base that you were born with. Hidden behind these innate talents are your highest values, which we will also look at. The connection between your natural talents base and your highest values means that when you are operating from the right Life Path, your Life Purpose will clearly emerge. The two things have a natural connection, and once you understand this, your life will become so much simpler and yet more rewarding!

In order to maintain the identity that is truly yours, you need to set some goals relating to your new life structure. To help keep you on track towards greater success in your career, there is a process for reconnecting with spirit, and hence your passion. We also look at daily techniques to help keep you focused and clear.

All over the world right now, there is great unrest in the workplace. Statistics show that many people are unhappy and frustrated with what they do, and with what they are *not* doing. Many of us have come to crisis points—like myself in the past—seeking out alternative employment, enrolling in courses, seminars, etc, desperately searching for more meaning in our lives. More often than not, idly hopping from one seminar to another is not only a waste of your precious time, but it actually increases your disappointment. So often, you can just end up choosing another course, another business or another seminar that is totally wrong for you!

Because people are unhappy, they seek out external solutions for their problems, trying to find that elusive 'ideal job', the next internet business, the next big adventure that will help them solve the conflict within. But evidence points to the fact that you carry your problems or issues of discontent *with you*, from job to job. The truth is, instead of looking for external solutions, you need to look *inside* for the source of the discontent that keeps coming up.

That is why this book focuses on connecting with your identity, because that is truly where the answer lies. And it's so much easier, so much more enjoyable than you may think! It's not just a quick fix or temporary solution—it's the kind of wonderful change that will be with you your whole life, and continue to change your life for the better.

If you have ever seen a happy person, then you know that they seem calm and content. They have a sense of self. They are centered and focused, concentrating their efforts in one area rather than scattering their energy and talents across a large range of activities. Sometimes their plans and successes seem to come about *effortlessly*. Sometimes everything they need seems to appear as if by magic. They seem to be luckier than you. Well, this is not the case. Luck has nothing to do with it! It's just that they have hit on all the right elements—they know who they are and what they should be doing and they are *doing that thing*. They are not wasting time and effort on things they are not meant to be doing.

Most of us land in jobs without having the time or information to really understand our Life Path. If a job or career is not satisfying to the individual soul, frustrations gradually build until we become totally stressed, unhappy and restless. If we just fall into the first job or career that comes along, we are most likely not on the right Life Path. Over time, we become deeply unhappy on a soul level. We have no idea of who we are or what contributions we can make. We don't know our highest values. We are unable to express those values in our work.

All of this leads to a very deep sense of unrest. This is when you see people changing jobs, thinking if they just change jobs again all will be well. But this is just the scatter-gun approach to solving the real problem. You may jump to another thing, hoping somehow you will land in the right spot, but how can you? In this situation, it's as if all you have is a vague map of life and you're throwing darts at it to pick a place to go—but then you have no actual idea of how to get there or why. Because you have no idea of where you actually are to begin with—no clear starting place. Not knowing who you are and what you're really, naturally good at keeps you in this strange limbo, this "non-place." So the key to making that life map less vague is to focus on connecting with your true identity, your true natural gifts and talents.

There are two routes to uncovering your true identity. In this edition, using a five-step blueprint to fast track your career success, we start the process off by understanding your spiritual identity. Through this approach, you can reconnect with your inner essence, your spirit, and let yourself be guided towards your innate skills and abilities. Or, you can take an easier, more direct path, by clarifying your career Life Path, and within that path, your innate skills and abilities. From there your highest values will emerge and then the right 'vehicle', the right job, career or business, will automatically appear. Either route works, and for many people it makes sense to combine the two. My purpose here is to give you a range of tools, so that you can choose what works most easily for you.

My aim in this edition is for you to take the easiest route to success in your career, first. Then, once you feel that you are on track again, and have a sense of purpose, you can take a deeper look at reconnecting with spirit. The wonderful thing is, if you find yourself on the right Life Path, you will *already* be in touch with spirit. This is when things feel in flow, when resources and decisions begin to come easily. Once it is 'easy', you will know that your spiritual and human life path are conjoined.

My five-step blueprint allows you to clarify both your spiritual and your human life identity. When you have clarity on both of these, and you are coming from a place of wholeness, you will be able to use all of your senses, all of your skills. Your intuition will be heightened. Your life will feel in sync; everything will feel as if it is in flow. You will be at one with your inner essence, your spirit.

You see, when you are overly stressed, or out of sync, you become restless and frustrated. It means you are not connected to your whole self. My goal for you by the end of this book is that you will have made a decision that you want to know yourself, your true identity, and that you make a commitment to yourself to take action towards that end. Because your work life occupies such a large chunk of time and energy, you will want to choose the Life Path that is right for you. You will want to uncover your innate skill and abilities. You will want to know your highest values and be able to express them fully in the right job, career or business.

In essence, *identity* is the key to fast track your career success. It is the key to greater self love, to greater passion and greater happiness in all areas of your life. This book contains all the tools you need to get closer to truly understanding your identity. There will be obstacles that try to throw you off track, like lack of love of self and others. This is normal—don't let it discourage you! Love *wants* to happen. Your success is waiting to happen! If you make a commitment to yourself to clarify who you are, to connect with your true identity, and to move forward on the Life Path that is right for you, then any lack of love in your life will be easily overcome.

I wish you every happiness in your adventure on the fast track to your career success.

From the Heart,
Trish Mackenzie

Contents

Chapter 1	Diamonds In The Rough: An Introduction To The Five Steps To Discovering Your Identity	17
Chapter 2	How To Make A Movie: My Story	29
Chapter 3	Reconnecting With Your Inner Self **Step 1**	43
Chapter 4	The Path Of Least Resistance **Step 2**, Part I	59
Chapter 5	There's Nobody Like You **Step 2**, Part II	79
Chapter 6	How To Guarantee Success In Every Area **Step 3**	93
Chapter 7	Forgiveness, The Miracle Key **Step 4**	105
Chapter 8	Colour My World (Daily Techniques) **Step 5**, Part I: Chakras	115
Chapter 9	Creating Forgiveness (Daily Techniques) **Step 5**, Part II: Tapping	127

Chapter 10 Turbo Charge Getting
           What You Want (Daily Techniques)
           Step 5, Part Iii: The Theta Mind 145

Chapter 11 Putting It All Together —
            A Blueprint For Success 161

Permissions And Resources Page 175

A Thank You Card For Someone Special 178

A Special Invitation 179

1

Diamonds in the Rough: an Introduction to the Five Steps

"An unexamined life is not worth living."
- **Socrates**

Looking over my life, there have certainly been times when I experienced the sweet thrill of success. On the other hand, it is just as easy to recall times when it seemed that no matter what I was doing, I was doomed to fail. Examining my unexamined life, certain things stand out now like giant, blinking signposts. Funny! How it's hard to see some things the first time around. Maybe we hide them from ourselves. Maybe sometimes we're so desperate to uncover the meaning of our existence we can't see the message that's right in front of us.

There is one thing that is always right in front of us, even though it may not feel like it—and that is love. Even in the darkest, most confused hour, love is our human birthright. It's waiting for us all the time, but all too often we build up walls to keep ourselves from seeing it. This book is about finding your way back to love.

Love shows up. It *wants* to show up. It wants to find us. Love is the natural state of things; and that's why it shows up when you are clear. When you are focused, directed, and following what has real meaning to you. The more settled and confident you feel that you are doing what you are meant to, the more love will come easily, naturally flooding into your life. You will see it in your work, in your relationships, your excitement to wake up in the morning. You will see it turn up naturally in the form of emotional and material riches. Following what has heart and meaning to you, you will reap the greatest possible rewards. This book is here to help you do that.

Have you ever noticed that love doesn't show up when you have no real direction in your life? If you're abusing yourself through substances or risky behaviours, if you hate your work, if you feel disconnected from yourself and those around you—it's a vicious cycle. We can actually get so used to *lack* of love that we think that's just the way life is. But it isn't. It doesn't have to be.

What if you could find the love you're missing? What if you had a clear path before you showing you exactly how to realise your dreams and contribute meaningfully to the world? What if you knew how to find the love of your life? These may sound like big promises. I assure you they are not.

The truth is surprisingly simple. I know this from my own experiences and I wrote this book to share my experiences with you. You can think of this book as your guide. With this guide, you can live a richer, fuller life immediately. A life filled with the love you deserve.

Here is basic truth number one: It is impossible to love yourself or anyone else unless you connect with yourself. Let me explain this a bit further. As humans, we have been disconnected from that which is truly meaningful. We've been cut off from our own spiritual purpose and we often have no clear idea *why* we are here. You know this feeling. You're not alone. I felt it most of my life and I'm here to tell you there is a way to reconnect.

People often say things like: "To thine own self be true" but they have no idea who they are. How can you be true to yourself if you don't know what you are being true to? Another thing you hear all the time is: "Do what you love!" But what if you don't know *what* it is that you love? This book will show you the way back—to your own source, and to the truth of what you love, to your passions. You will find your way back to loving yourself. And only from there can you truly love others and live the life you deserve.

I'm going to talk about something called a Life Path—this is what you are going to find as you read this book. I have capitalised this expression because, yes, there is just one that is yours. It belongs to you. It's waiting for you. You don't have to invent your Life Path—you only have to uncover it. Later in the book, I'll give you some tools for uncovering the Life Path that is yours and, through it, your life purposes.

You'll know you've uncovered your Life Path when you feel a sense of flow. That's something I'm going to be talking about a lot throughout this book. It's the feeling of being connected to your true self and acting *from that place*. When you do, life really does flow. It moves along smoothly. It *feels* right. Almost effortless!

Almost effortless, I say, because I am going to talk about some things that will require a bit of effort on your part. But the effort only lies in keeping a daily practice to make sure that you stay in contact with your true identity. The practice will come easily, once you have found your way back to the truest, deepest part of yourself.

The reason that life will begin to feel effortless is that you will clarify your natural talents. This is another fundamental truth: Those little things you do naturally, the talents that come so easily to you that you don't think of them as "real" skills—those are your resources. When you figure out and acknowledge what those are your life will begin to change *immediately*. You will have the sense that you are being seen for the first time, that you are finally being accepted and understood for *who you are*. You will also begin to reconnect with your passions. You will feel joy and love for yourself and others for no reason.

In my experience, *The Secret* and other books that focus on the "Laws of Attraction" tend to gloss over how to attract more substance, meaning, and purpose into your life and what to do when faced with adversity. They put forth the idea that we must change negative thinking patterns and only put positive thoughts out there. That's true, but I also think that the real story is what these authors are doing behind the scenes. It's the fact that they had clarified *who they were*, and were operating from the right Life Path that allowed their natural talents to shine through. This is the place from which you attract more abundance, more inner and outer wealth—and that's what my book is going to focus on.

Once you clarify your identity and start using your natural talents, the talents you were born with, life will begin to flow. You will begin to attract abundance in all areas of your life. This is *just what happens* when you are aligned with your inner self. It simply is.

My Background Story

I always felt isolated and different from others, not only among my work group and friends, but even within my family. I struggled all my life to find that 'something' that would keep me interested— something that would give meaning to my life. Like many people, I was waiting for that "Aha!" moment, when everything would become clear. I did all the usual things in my quest: I attended seminars and self-development talks and read a number of self-help books, constantly on the look-out for that "one thing" that would jump out and bite me on the nose. But it never did.

Well, it's hard to recognise the "one thing" if you don't really know what you are looking for. I realise now that what I really needed was a spiritual explanation for my existence on this planet. I couldn't see how I *fit* anywhere. Why was I here?

It's really no wonder that I would ask myself these questions given the environment that I grew up in. My childhood home was not a place where I felt safe. It was not a place of support or nurturing or love because my parents didn't know how to create that environment. Like so many parents, they were just mimicking what their own parents had done. They had no role models themselves. No one in the family had any real direction or set goals. It seemed there was no purpose for any of us. The only thing we had in abundance was criticism.

I guess this is probably a 'normal' background for someone with a Catholic upbringing. We learnt about fear, doubt, judgment, sin and guilt. I had low self-esteem and little confidence. I was averse to any kind of risk-taking. The God I learnt about was punishing. We learnt that we would go to hell. I did not understand why we Catholics were the only ones who were going to heaven. That didn't make sense to me. There was a state of constant duality—good, bad, right, wrong, sin and punishment. I never understood why a loving God would sanction all this. What better way to create a pattern of circular, negative thinking? I now recognise that during periods of languishing in this negativity trap, I have in the past slipped back into old habits—habits of failure and lack.

I have found that if 'success' habits are not securely ingrained then it is easy to slip back into old bad habits. Even though I was always on the lookout for "the answer," I was still going through periods of failure. And the periods of failure became longer. The periods of success in between became shorter. I felt hopeless, as if I were doomed to repeat the same mistakes over and over forevermore. My lack of direction and focus condemned me to an "almost life." You see, I had lost my connection to my true identity and I was unable to find my way back to love.

During this time, I kept asking my higher self for help, for direction. I knew somehow that this was an answer. This was my saviour. I kept asking how I could find success again.

Then the "hallelujah!" moment arrived in the form of a book. *A Return to Love* by Marianne Williamson outlines how the author overcame struggle by welcoming the concept of *forgiveness* into her life. Marianne adopted the principle of forgiveness because she, in turn, had read a book called *A Course in Miracles*. At first, I hesitated to read *A Course in Miracles* because it appeared religious; the word "God" permeated the book. Of course, given my background, I associated this word with organised religion—something I didn't entirely trust.

I'm glad my curiosity finally won out, though, because I now understand something very important: *A Course in Miracles* is the basis of the Christian faith. However, it is not meant to be organised into a religion. It's about how we are, what we do, and why we do things. It's about our separation from spirit and from our own higher purpose. It's about regaining love, for ourselves and for others.

My book is not about religion either. It's about finding love again. It's about finding your essence, your true self. It is about finding your identity and your purpose. This is the truest and deepest part of you and, once there, everything will fall into place. You will know that you have come home.

You will no longer need to look for "things" to make you happy. Once you have identified your Life Path, you will be able to clarify who you are within it. Along with this, your true life purposes will emerge because you will be connected with both your spiritual self *and* your human self. From this place of connection, your life will unfold with seemingly endless offerings—new opportunities, healthier relationships, and simple moments of joy.

I discovered that the steps were very clear and easy to follow. I want to share them with you to provide you with a fast track way of securing the rich, and meaningful life that you deserve. My objective is to shortcut your time to success based on the time that I wasted in my efforts to succeed.

Overall, I'm simply an ordinary person who has decided to have a go. You see, there was a time when I was on the verge of becoming an overnight success, but I literally "forgot" the mechanics of how to do that. The time I had my greatest success was when I made a movie. All the elements of success were in place. I had built the spiritual foundation and had the inner connection that I needed. I had the quality framework and the direction of my Life Path. Because I had clearly defined my role *within* that Life Path, my purpose and my natural talents came to the fore and I was using them to their best advantage. I had set the goals and I was using daily techniques. I was operating from a place of love. My identity was clearly defined. *However, I did not know at the time that I was in the right Life Path.* Because all of the elements were in place everything came to me easily. This is what will happen for you when you follow these five steps and define your identity.

I was totally focused. I was totally disciplined, and there was nothing that could get in my way to complete this film. It came from a place of 'knowing' that I would achieve my goal. In essence, I was in a place of theta mind the whole time, as opposed to beta, the normal mind, which I will explain later.

However, within two years of completing the movie, I literally 'forgot' the steps. I was out of the 'success' environment. I lost my sense of direction. I changed to a different life path and it was the wrong one for me. So what happened? I lost my identity. I lost my connection with my inner self. I fell into a negativity trap. This time it was a big one and I had no idea how to get out of it. Failure seemed ingrained in my cells.

The constant chattering of the beta mind or the ego mind was in full play. It was as though I was destined to fail. I could not lift myself out of this valley of despair. During that period in the negativity trap, I had this huge nagging sense of not belonging. It was though I was dumped on the wrong planet and I was still waiting for someone to pick me up. Unfortunately they never came.

Friends and family turned against me. I kept running out of money trying different things to bring me back to that success. The things that I was going for were combinations of different business ideas that were totally against my natural skills. This meant that it was something I needed to 'learn,' some new skill, rather than building on my natural talents.

When I did the movie everything came easily and naturally. When things come easily it is difficult to see that these natural talents are recognisable skills. As a result, I was unable to capitalise on my success at the time.

Once I re-connected with my Higher Self, though, opportunities just began popping up. I no longer had to seek them out. Articles, books, seminars, helpful people and techniques simply began to *find me*. The opportunity to write a book found me. I no longer feel isolated. Now, I have a true sense of belonging, and it came via the principle of forgiveness. It came through the daily techniques that I use. It came because I finally recognised my true identity, and I was able to release my anger, resentment and bitterness. I felt, instead, the stirrings of strength and success.

I asked my spirit to send me my life purpose, and spirit obliged. Essentially, this is the story of an unexamined life that radically changed into a life where I can reach others. For myself as much as for you, I want to share my shortcuts to success. I want to help you avoid the pitfalls, if I can, that I used to fall into.

Ultimately, this book is about finding your way back to loving yourself, no matter what you have been through, so that you can truly begin to love others. To do this, you have to find your true identity. I'll go into the steps in more detail later in the book, but for now here is an overview.

Finding your identity is like building a house.

Step 1: Establish your foundation.

First, you need a solid foundation—a stable, grounded place from which to conduct your life. This is going to be a spiritual foundation; that is, your connection with your inner self. In order to have a stable place to work from, it's essential that you first connect with *who you really are*. So often on earth, we suffer from the feeling that we are disconnected from God, from our spiritual source. Essentially, what this translates to is that we are not connected with ourselves. If you understand your spiritual purpose here on earth, then it's easy to see that we really are all one. We are all one with the divine—and this divinity wants good things for us. If we have this as a foundation, the next step is easy.

Step 2: Discover your framework- identity

Once you have established a spiritual foundation, you can start constructing a concrete framework for your *human self*. I will use this expression throughout the book as a way of talking about your existence as an embodied person, in this world now. You see, we all have both a spiritual self and a human self. Keeping these aspects in communication with one another is an important element of discovering your framework. That's why being in touch with your Higher Self helps you stay on the right Life Path.

The first aspect of discovering your framework is to identify your Life Path. As I said earlier, you only have one true Life Path—you just have to uncover it. In Chapter 4, I'll go into more detail on how this is done. This Life Path is the bare bones of your framework, and from it will emerge your life purposes. As you go through the process of clarifying who you are, finding your identity and identifying your natural talents, and reconnecting with your passions, you'll be able to see these life purposes easily. They will be in line with your natural talents and with who you really are. You will feel validated and understood. The passions within will begin to stir.

Part of building the framework is to identify which rooms are to be used for what purpose. Accordingly, this is where you define your purpose/s. Building a framework is about getting to know yourself and putting your individual stamp on each room. Because you will be using your natural talents, your own true gifts, you will have the maximum ability to generate abundance in your life. You will be doing what you are good at and what you love.

Step 3: Construct your boundary

Every house needs a fence: in this case, that means goals. The boundary is the fence that contains your whole house—what goes on in the house, what goes on in the yard. Having found your true Life Path and hence life purpose/s, which match your natural talents and your passions, and having clarified your unique talents within that framework, you can then write and set meaningful goals. You are more likely to achieve these goals, as they will now be relevant to your true Life Path and Life Purpose/s, will work around your passions and with what you are naturally good at. Your true identity. You will be doing what you love and loving what you do.

Step 4: Protect your house; an umbrella of love.

This part springs from Step 1. In fact, the umbrella of love for all of the other steps is the key tool of *forgiveness*. If we understand that we are all one and that God loves us all equally, and we practice forgiveness at every opportunity, then we will come to see others and ourselves as equals. We will come to understand love: love of ourselves *and* love of others. So you see, it really is—actually, about love!

Step 5: Keep your house in order.

What's the use of building the perfect house if you leave it messy all the time? Taking care of yourself and staying on track requires a bit of daily practice. In light of this, there are several daily techniques that you can use to achieve your goals more easily. These will help you stay connected to spirit and help you clear away limiting information and beliefs. This is one area that may change or increase over time. You might add other techniques as you become more successful and confident, or adapt them as you see fit to better keep you on track.

Part of the journey to self-discovery is via self-examination. In the next chapter, I will examine a successful period of my life—the making of my movie. This is not to say that you have to make a movie, of course! I'm just using this as a blueprint to demonstrate what elements were operating during this period of success in my life. This will help you recognise a structure, a pattern that you can use as a foundation for the rest of your successful life—the life you deserve! Knowing this structure will fast track your career success.

How to Make a Movie: My Story

"I couldn't wait for success. So I went ahead without it."
— **Jonathan Winters**

I'm going to examine a period in my life when—even though I didn't quite know it at the time—I was on the right Life Path and *everything* had flow. In Chapter 1, I gave you an overview of the five steps to living the life you deserve. Now, I'm going to show you how those five steps applied directly to this successful period in my life. Please remember, the success that came out of this period in my life came from the fact that I was using my *natural base talents*, the little gifts that are a part of my true identity. When this happens, often what we are doing doesn't even feel like work, so you may not associate such periods of time with success or being on the right path. Most likely, that's exactly when *you are*.

I want you to think back over your life and recall a time when you were doing something that felt *right*, a period when things just seemed to flow. This could be related to school, career, family—or it could just be a fun project you did at some time in the past. Hopefully you can call to mind a period of success like this, but even if you can't—please don't worry! Before you finish reading this book, you will know what I mean.

When your life is in flow, it seems as if everything you need just *arrives* suddenly—like magic. You attract what you want, exactly when you need it. Natural talents build on each other and you begin to *see* what you are good at. Generally, what you're really good at are not learned skills—they're things you do *naturally*. When you operate from this place, your attractiveness increases—people want to be around you. They can sense the good, positive energy coming from you. You *automatically* gather the best people you need to help you out. More and more, you feel you are coming from a place of *knowing* rather than hoping you are or doubting your ability. You *know* that you *will* achieve whatever you have set your mind on. I have discovered that when those periods occur in life it's because, whether we are aware of it or not, the five steps I outlined in Chapter 1 are *already operating*. If you think back on a successful period, you can identify the ways in which those five steps were operating, and you can use this information to build that structure again for future endeavours. I'm going to use my own success story as an example to show you how this works.

How I Made a Movie

Part 1: Why Not?

Having spent most of my adult life as an accountant, the idea of making a movie when I think about it now seems almost insane! I had been a tutor, a lecturer and a principal of my own accounting firm— but those occupations are all a far cry from movie producer. Keep this in mind: sometimes what you *should* be doing looks very different from what you *are* doing. It may take a leap of faith, and it may come from an unexpected place. How did

I decide to make a movie? Well, I met a guy in a bar—and the rest, as they say, is history. It just seemed like a good idea at the time!

I started out by researching all I could about the film industry and reading movie scripts. We decided to write our own script and, much like our relationship, it wasn't very good. But even though that relationship—both business and personal—went sour, I was hooked on the idea of making a movie. Instead of letting the idea go and giving into the self-doubting mind, I thought to myself, "Why not?" I held onto the story idea and was determined to move ahead with it.

You see, **Step 1 (building a foundation)** was already at work here—even though I wasn't fully aware of it. At this time in my life, I was also enrolled in a Higher Consciousness Course. That two-year course helped me build my *spiritual foundation*. I wasn't feeling isolated or disconnected at the time, so the doubting mind was quiet. I was connected to myself, and that's what allowed me to say, "Why not make a movie?" I took advice from my Higher Self and my Higher Self was saying, "Hey, you're not only an accountant—you can make a movie, too." I listened.

Part 2: The Film Course

I really had *no idea* how to make a movie. But a large part of following your nature is saying "Just have a go!" So I did. Undeterred by my ignorance, I enrolled in a 12 week film course that covered basic elements like how to work a camera, what the various roles like director and producer mean, and some basics on script writing, sound and editing. Most of this, honestly, was too technical for me. I was caught up in the idea of making a movie and that's what I kept focusing on.

When it came time to form groups to make our film, no one wanted to take on the role of producer. I volunteered. This was perfect for me—and I already had a script. The only problem was that it was a full feature film script. Editing it down to something manageable, and keeping the integrity of the story intact, was a minor hump. For this reason, my first film was just under 20 minutes, instead of the six minutes that everyone else was making. Part of my nature is that I have trouble thinking small.

So, making a longer first film did not faze me. You see, I was moving through **Step 2 (discovering my Life Path)** almost effortlessly and with excitement. By taking the film course and learning the basics that I needed to make my movie, I was building my framework, getting the tools I would need to stay on my Life Path. At this phase, my purpose was evolving from *within*. I knew that I was the moviemaker, so my purpose was clearly defined. I was clarifying who I was for myself, and that meant discovering natural talents I didn't know I had—such as producing a film of almost 20 minutes for my first go around! I allowed my natural talents to evolve because I was in the flow and I accepted whatever came along.

This idea of staying in the flow carries over to the next step as well. As you'll see, being in tune with your Higher Self, finding your Life Path, your purpose and clarifying your natural talents base and acting from that place of love naturally increases your attractiveness—so that people are drawn to you, and they *want* to work with you and be around you. This was essential for the next phase, where I built my boundary by defining my goals.

Part 3: Keeping the Ball Rolling

I knew that I could inspire and motivate people. I knew that I often improvised my way through life. However, to what extent

I had these skills I would never have known if I hadn't put myself in the way of new experiences. Making my movie was certainly that—and I needed to get the right team. Many of those in our group who were budding cameramen and potential editors or sound techs were obviously put out when the teachers suggested that, in order to make our film more professional, perhaps they—the teachers—should do these jobs. But this gave me an idea.

This is another aspect of my nature that I learned to trust—I see the bigger picture, the overview. I thought to myself, "Why not ask professional, established movie makers to help with the film?" Sure, they could say "no." But what if they said "yes?" It wouldn't hurt to try.

So, that's what I did. I found lists of professional moviemakers in various categories and asked a smattering of people right at the top of their profession, some in the middle, and some first timers. Remember, all I had in mind was that making a movie sounded like a good idea. It also seemed fun. I had a script. I went to film school. Of course these professional people would take notice of me!

Here's where **Step 3 (building your boundary)** was happening for me. From my original idea, I *developed a goal* that I was going to make this movie, no matter what. Who was going to be involved? I had to figure that out. That was part of the goal setting, too. But I had my script and my idea and I felt I was ready. Sure, this seemed totally nuts at the time—a person with absolutely no experience in the field calling up professionals and asking if they'd help me make my film for FREE! But this is the wonderful thing—*I just thought I would succeed.* Because I had no experience in this field, I had no experience of failure embedded in my DNA. I had absolutely no concept that I would fail. I figured that I would ask people and someone would say "yes!" So, I set my goal and went about the task of finding my professional team.

I sent out over a hundred very simple emails to cameramen/women (DOP's, directors of photography) in various tiers of their profession. This is what I wrote, verbatim: "I am doing a short film with a film school and need a DOP. Can you please help here? Many thanks."

I had 37 responses to this email from people involved at all levels. Some had worked on major films overseas and asked if I could wait as they were in New York or Los Angeles and would be back later. However, the first response that I got was from one of Australia's top DOP's, Ian Jones. Ian is highly qualified and has made award- winning movies such as *Tracker*, *Rabbit Proof Fence* and *Ten Canoes*, which went on to great acclaim at the Cannes Film Festival. Ian's response to my email? Simply, "Happy to help out, tell me more."

Can you imagine that?! He was a guy after my own heart. A man of few words who just got to the point! Of course at that stage I was jumping around for joy, and I was *buoyed on to further success*. This is the relevant point here—success builds upon success. As I was setting my goals, in the flow, coming from a place of *knowing*, and being *accidentally* on the right Life Path, using my natural talents base, I just *knew* I *would* succeed—everything was falling into place.

Long story short? Ian and I met and he quickly agreed to do the movie. Not only that, he brought his wife, Karen Mahood, on board as first assistant director. I still needed an editor and with Ian and Karen on board, I felt confident in setting my sights on David Stiven, who had edited one of Australia's most successful films, *Crocodile Dundee*.

David's response went as follows: "Wow! Well I'm almost exhausted but enthused by your enthusiasm. I am a film editor... some of my major credits... include: *Crocodile Dundee* and *Mad Max ll*... please contact me for a chat... And of course I would be able to cut your short film."

So, we now had three of the most professional and senior filmmakers in Australia signed on, for FREE, mind you. When I told Ian Jones my budget, which was approximately $2600, I was expecting that he might think I was nuts. He probably did. But he never told me this to my face. Instead, my goals kept getting accomplished one by one—because I was staying in touch with my true purpose. David even introduced me to one of the top line producers in the country, Sue Mackay, and she called in some other professional people to do the sound and the editing. All of these people agreed to come on board for free.

I had originally intended to shoot the film on a hand held video camera, as prescribed in the film course. However, Ian said that he wanted to shoot on film, and so I agreed. What could I do? He knew what he was doing. I had no idea. During my discussions with all of the professionals on my team, I spoke with such confidence and was so focused on what I wanted to achieve, they all thought I knew more than I did. I did have to keep reminding Ian about that.

As you may have observed, one of my particular *natural base talents* is—improvising! Also, I tend to *think big* when I am operating from a place of flow. Now, when I say this I'm not suggesting that you have to go about things in your life in the same way I have. What is most important is that you discover what *your* natural base talents are and keep in touch with your Higher Self in order to stay in the flow. And later in the book I'll give you some tools for finding your own natural base talents.

At this point, I was keeping a daily practice of asking my Higher Self to help me out so that the people, resources, and money I needed would appear. This is where **Step 5 (keeping your house in order)** was naturally coming into play. I was using daily techniques, which I will explain later in the book, to clear any negative energy from my aura. I maintained my focus via guided meditation. All of these things allowed me to continue operating from my true identity, kept my attitude positive and kept me connected to my Higher Self. Once you are connected to your Higher Self, you are effectively coming from a place called the theta mind. This is the place where you can access all *known and unknown* information and ask for help from your Higher Self to send you the resources, people, money, knowledge—*anything* that you require to achieve your goals. I first learned this process via a two-year course, and via techniques that we used daily to clear our auras and chakras. Now, I am not suggesting that you enroll in such a course. In fact, my reason for writing this book is to give you the shortcut! I have since found an easier method for you to achieve theta mind and have access to the wealth of the universe. You'll find this technique—and others that I use daily to maintain positive energy—in the chapters on daily techniques.

Back to the story of the film! Now, the way in which I obtained the camera that Ian Jones wanted as well as a cast of actors is proof positive of the effectiveness of **keeping your house in order**. I said that if you stay in contact with your Higher Self, all the resources you need will *come to you*. It's absolutely true. So how did I get a great cast of actors? They were crawling out of the woodwork because I had managed to get so many top-of-the-industry professionals on board already.

How did I get the expensive cameras Ian Jones wanted to shoot the film? I asked Panavision for them, and they gave them to me *for free*. That's right. Armed with a recent story a journalist had done on my film, I met with the head executive of Panavision and asked for a camera. I said it was "because Ian Jones wants one"—and it worked. Not only that, he asked me if I needed any sound equipment or *anything else to help me out*. It was like a one-stop shop for all the equipment I needed to make my film, at no cost to me.

This is simply what happens when you follow the steps—what you need comes to you. And this will happen for you once you have all the steps lined up. Now, in the next section, we'll jump backwards a bit to Step 4. I've put this one last because really it comes before, during and after all the other steps. And the need for this crucial step—*forgiveness*—becomes especially clear when you are confronted with challenges on your Life Path. And when I was making my movie, there certainly were challenges. But I kept the umbrella of love up over everything, and that's why this is a success story.

Part 4: Umbrella of Love

So, I had my production side of things sorted out, I had a cast of actors, and the locations, costumes and food were all coming together. Now—God knows why!—I decided I wanted a big song and dance number during the credits roll at the end of the film. I just did. So, now I had to organise for a songwriter, musicians, singers—goodness! This looked like it was getting out of hand, but one idea just created the next and I knew I had to go with it.

I enlisted a friend, an opera singer, to help write the two original songs. I had in mind a very particular beat. I just felt that it had to be that way. And I trusted myself because I was operating from the theta mind I mentioned previously. I just kept up my daily practice and stayed in the flow. Gordon Costello came up with two very lovely tunes for me. He also composed some score music throughout the film, and adapted some particular music for a couple of scenes.

Then, the lyricist I thought was coming on board pulled out. So, guess what? I decided to do it myself. How hard could it be? I had never written lyrics to a song before, but then I had never produced a film before either! And here I was doing that. So, why not? Thus 'O bar blues' was born. And I wrote the other song, 'Town hero', for the final scene as well. I just believed I could, and I did. Then, lo and behold, one of my singers dropped out. So I stepped in and did her job, too. You can see the pattern here. If someone dropped out I would fill the gap. I even tried to find a professional director along the way but they were in short supply—so I did it myself! I improvised my way through every aspect of this film. However, as you will discover in a later chapter, this was one of my *natural base talents*. If in doubt, just make it up as you go along!

Now! There were a couple of other problems along the way. But, with **Step 4 (forgiveness; the umbrella of love)** firmly in place, I chose not to see them as problems—just minor hiccups designed to throw me off track. I think the universe does that sometimes, just to see if you really mean to achieve what you set out to do. My first production manager quit because she decided that she wanted to be paid. I just found another one. And when she could no longer do the job, either? You guessed it, I just did it myself! I also had a production assistant who was a trainee learning the ropes. For some reason he misinterpreted something that I said and decided to opt out. But I was so focused that *failure was not an option*. I forgave these people in my heart and pressed on. Because I was only operating from a place of love, I was able to do that. Any ill wishes or problems coming my way just bounced right off of me. I figured that people self-select. If they choose to be on board, great! If not, too bad.

The most problematic matter that I had was that I had no sound two days before the shoot, as all the sound technicians I had found wanted to be paid. I finally had to agree to pay someone to do sound just to keep things running. Unfortunately, he told the rest of the team and I nearly had a mutiny. I decided that he would need to come on board for free, just like everyone else. Part of my natural talents base is my ability to inspire and motivate people. So, this is what I had to do with this guy. Guess what! He came on board for free! He even ended up by saying that he had the most fun on this movie. By the way, the movie is called *The Rip-Off*. It's a comedy in the style of *Faulty Towers*, which was the all-time classic for nutty behaviour. John Cleese is a favourite.

Now, the other possible major disaster was that the lead actress suddenly decided that she was not going to come to any more rehearsals. Because our locations for the major scenes were so far apart, we had to shoot over the weekends. I had organised a further rehearsal as well for the song and dance routine, but the actress decided she wasn't going to attend. At this stage, we had already started filming and this could have been disastrous! But I listened to what she had to say. I kept the umbrella of love up. I made the quickest decision of my life. I told her that she had five minutes to decide whether she would do what was expected—or let the rest of the cast down.

It worked. She agreed to stay on and come to the rehearsals. But, after I thought about this for a couple of days, I had to sack her anyway. It was a tough decision, but I realized that as a director I really needed to trust my actors, and I could no longer really trust her.

Sometimes on your Life Path you have to make difficult decisions—but if you are coming from a place of love, of forgiving yourself and others, you will make the right decision. Long story short, we had a great shoot. Don't get me wrong—plenty of other interesting situations arose! Like when Ian Jones decided he needed one more camera and I had to go back to Panavision and ask for another one for free! Well, we got it. Then there was the editing—going through all those rolls of film and making sure the colours matched. And syncing up all the music. And adding extra background dialogue and nature sounds. But no matter what came up—I was covered by the umbrella of love so nothing seemed like a disaster to me. And it wasn't. We made a professional film, one I can be proud of.

You see, no matter what mishaps came up along the way, I refocused on what I wanted. I kept focusing on who I was, and any negativity just dissipated. Easily. When you are in flow, you attract all manner of resources—people, places, events and experiences. You are in sync with yourself. That means forgiving yourself and those around you for any mistakes or bumps in the road.

Your natural birthright is to experience joy and love, not hardship and lack. So, when you find yourself out of sync with joy and love—*you have to forgive yourself for an error in your thinking*, either about yourself or someone else. You may be holding a grudge or being cruel to yourself—this will impair your ability to attract and manifest. Using the tool of forgiveness—for yourself and for others—you will always find your way back to your *true* essence. And that is love.

In telling you the story of making my movie, I hope you can see clearly that there were five steps at work to create the success I had. Success breeds success. It stems from using your natural talents, doing what you love and coming from a place of love. Now, if you're not sure yet what your natural base talents are, don't worry. In Chapter 4, you'll find out how you can find your Life Path and clarify your identity and your purpose. You don't have to make a film, like I did, but you will have the opportunity to make the movie of your own life. In this movie, everyone will come on board with you. What you need will show up for you. Everyone will say "yes!"

To begin with, we will look at finding your spiritual path, your rock—a foundation from which to guide the rest of your life.

3

Reconnecting with Your Inner Self

"Your work is to discover your work and then with all your heart to give yourself to it."

— **Buddha**

Step 1: Establish Your Spiritual Foundation

Step 1 of the 5 steps to living the life you deserve is to establish your spiritual foundation. Now, this does not necessarily mean choosing a religion. As I have already mentioned, I am myself skeptical of "organised religion" and I understand such skepticism in others. To be clear, what I mean by *establishing your spiritual foundation* is to reconnect with your inner essence, your true self. From our human perspective here on earth, there is a fundamental underlying feeling of being separated from God—which can also be described as our *inner essence*. Yes, we have been separated, but the truth is that we are all one. So this step is about understanding the way the separation feels, how it shows up in your life, and then getting back to the place of wholeness—where you understand your spiritual purpose.

When we are coming from this place of separation, we experience a profound *lack of love*. There is a lack of love on a deep, soul level, and it shows up in our lives as a sense of restlessness, of not belonging. We feel disconnected from ourselves and those around us. We feel that we don't *fit in* anywhere. It can feel as if you were dumped on the wrong planet, only to wait a lifetime for "them" to come pick you up—only you don't even know who "they" are. So of course they never came!

As humans, this lack of love shows up as having no meaningful purpose, no life direction, no focus, no clarity. You are out of sync with your *natural birthright*, which is happiness and joy. As I said in the beginning of the book, love wants to show up. It is the natural state of things. *Lack* of love shows up when you are angry, and resentful, carrying and holding onto bitterness and old pain, unable to shake free.

I know these feelings because I experienced them for much of my life. I was always hoping for a miracle—something that would end my sense of isolation, something that would take away the sense that I didn't *belong* here. I felt alone. I had no sense of attachment to the planet, to this place I found myself. I didn't even feel any joy in securing material things. It was as if nothing was real anyway—I was adrift in a sea of meaninglessness. My life was far from rich and fulfilling. All I knew was a constant compulsion to search for *a place to belong*.

What did I do to fill the void? The usual things: alcohol, food, sex, seminars, more seminars, more attempts at healing. This only led to a sense of further isolation and retreat from many areas in my life. I had a sense of quiet desperation that I would never achieve my potential. There was lack everywhere in my life. And I did not know how to overcome this.

As I mentioned in Chapter 1, an innate sense that Marianne Williamson's *A Return to Love* was where I needed to go. But I was deeply hesitant because of my early negative associations with organised religion. I was untrusting of the concept of a so-called God, and I was reluctant to look there for my answers. But my desperate feeling wouldn't go away, and I finally bought the book *A Course in Miracles*.

At times, it was hard to read because of my mistrustful relationship to the concept of a Christian God, but I did find the answer I was looking for. This book showed me *why* I felt such a deep feeling of not belonging, of being adrift and unconnected to self, to work, to the planet, and to others. It described "the separation"—what it meant to be a *spirit* essentially, yet having a human experience on this planet. I suddenly understood my reason for being here on this planet—and I understood why it had been so hard for me to feel any sense of connection before. Once you understand the reason for your feeling of disconnection, it becomes easy to find your way back to connection with spirit, to a *meaningful* human existence. And from here, your Life Path and your life purposes will pop up for you.

So, this chapter is about understanding your spiritual foundation so that you can then move forward to reconnection with your inner essence, your spirit. So, I am going to talk about the concept of your *spiritual identity* and why you are here. I'm also going to talk about what we as humans do to each other to throw each other off, and how it is possible to live a more meaningful human life.

To provide a background for these concepts, I'm going to give you an overview of what I found so illuminating from *A Course in Miracles* (*ACIM*). If, like me, you do not consider yourself religious in the traditional sense, I want to make it clear that *this is not a religious discourse. ACIM* is a way to help us find our spiritual purpose here on earth. It explains our deep feeling of isolation and separation, and it gives us the tools we need to live out that spiritual purpose—and to move forward in our lives from our *natural state of love and connection.*

For those who are unfamiliar with *ACIM*, the dialogue was channeled to a person named Helen Schucman. It took many years for Helen and her colleague to transcribe the information and make it available for public use. There is now a school to help people come to grips with this ground breaking information. The school is run by a group called Foundation for Inner Peace.

ACIM points out that God did not mean for us to have separate religions. It is essentially an expose designed to correct a misunderstanding about the story of Jesus, to end suffering, and to find forgiveness, atonement, and the meaning of the crucifixion. I will not go into great detail about *ACIM*, per se, but I would like to outline some of the basic premises. These teachings are incredibly useful as a starting point for finding meaning for the concept of *soul and spirit*. Finding personal meaning for these terms is essential for you to reconnect with your inner essence and find your true spiritual identity. *ACIM* examines many things that we are most probably doing now—if we are in a disconnected state—and describes ways to view the world so that we can shift our perception. Once we make this shift, we can understand what is really happening in our bodies as humans and begin to live life with purpose

The basic teaching at the heart of *ACIM* is this: *Our only problem, as humans, is our belief that we have "separated" from God.* (If, as I was initially, you are uncomfortable with the word "God," feel free to insert the term "Source Mind" or something you are more comfortable with here). All our spiritual and human problems stem from this one error. If we can correct that via a change of perception then we can live simply and meaningfully. *ACIM* also gives us an overriding tool to use throughout the rest of our lives that can guide us back to our natural birthright—one of love, peace and joy.

Now, let me provide a little background as to how this "separation" arose in the first place. God-who is said to be changeless, timeless, and all creative—wanted to share these qualities with another. Therefore, he created his son, Christ. Christ was endowed with the same aspects and creative qualities of The Father. However, he had one additional aspect as well—a Will. This meant that Christ could choose to do what he liked, when and why he so chose. When *ACIM* refers to the person named Christ, it is also referring to **mankind**. So when they talk about the Son of God, they are talking about we humans.

For some unknown reason, Christ decided that he wanted to do things differently from The Father, so he "separated" from God. Essentially, this was really only a distancing from God, because what God has created cannot actually be separate from him completely. What Christ's "separation" created was the Ego Mind—or the Wrong Mind. I also relate this to the Beta Mind; it is the mind that attaches to negativity, fear, doubt, judgment, criticism, anger and false perceptions. When Christ created the Ego Mind, God, in his infinite wisdom, knew that from then on, mankind would have a struggle throughout life. To help mankind in its struggle, he created what is called the Holy Spirit, the Right Mind. This Right Mind *is our avenue to return to love*, to reconnect with our *true inner selves*. The Holy Spirit is our direct link back to God. In today's world we call it the Higher Self. So, in order to find our way back to God we need to reconnect with our Higher Self, the Holy Spirit.

Now, this is crucial to understand: the "separation" is really *only a thought* —an illusion. The Ego Mind is also a thought. We can *change our minds* and create right-minded thinking. It's all a matter of choice. When the thought of separation arose, Christ created the Ego Mind and, within it, feelings of guilt for separating from God. The Ego Mind also created feelings of fear and lack. In the Ego Mind, we experience *a lack of love* — because of Christ's (mankind's) separation from God (Source Mind). In essence, negativity is man-made—it's just a thought. Change your mind, and you will change your reality. You will begin to live in the *real world*.

Underlying Christ's decision to separate from God is a feeling of deep, irreconcilable guilt for having done so. The Garden of Eden story is one version of this guilt-tale. When Adam and Eve partook of the Forbidden Fruit, they were then banished to wander the planet trying to find their way back to salvation. The Forbidden Fruit is the decision that Christ took to separate from God. Wandering the planet in constant search for a way back to God, to love, outlines the journey that the rest of mankind must take until we all see the light.

This also means that God did not "create" the universe. Christ—*mankind*—did. You have to ask, why would a God who is all loving, changeless, and timeless create such a world as we know today – a world of floods, famine, poverty, murder, sin, victimisation and punishment. The answer is that *God did not create this*. We inherited the ability to create from him, and we have gone about doing so from a misguided perception—the perception that we are now *separated* from God. In essence, this is not possible. So, mankind is languishing in a hell here on earth, *all because of a misperception*. Because the misperception is built on the foundation of our guilt, this guilt underlies everything we do, everything we perceive, every action we take here on earth.

This means that the perspective of our whole lives is based on a false premise. We still feel guilty, no matter what. We perceive everything based on this false perception. Because of our underlying guilt we attempt to "hide" our guilt by perceiving others as "wrong," or saying that they have "sinned against us." In God's world *there is no sin*. He calls any misdemeanours *errors*, errors of perception. In fact, *Man* created sin and punishment in order to alleviate his sense of guilt. Instead of correcting our perception, mankind *projects onto others his own guilt*. We see wrong in others—it is they who have sinned. We do this all the time. We blame others for sinning against us. We claim a right to feel angry and victimised. We enlist others to agree with us. We have set up rules and laws in order to perpetuate this sense of being sinned against.

Now, it is important to note that, according to *ACIM*, when spirits come to earth to have a human life experience, they have all *agreed to the rules and laws of the land* prior to coming here. This means that, as spirits, we have accepted the idea of separation, the notion of guilt, the misperceptions, and the practice of *projection*. Projection is the process whereby, because of own underlying sense of guilt, we cast onto others all manner of events so that the other person is seen as the guilty one. Our judicial system is based on this notion. Thus, we all continue to play the game unknowingly.

ACIM explains the "separation" so that we can know this important truth: *we really are not separated from God*. It is merely our *misperception* that we have been separated from God, spirit, love. ACIM asks us to look at what we perceive in the world around us as a way of unraveling the nonsense that is happening. Only by doing this can we find our way back to God. And God maintains his connection with us through snippets of *insight from our Higher Selves.*

ACIM asks us not only to understand the notion of separation but also to *re-examine all of our perceptions*. We live based on our perceptions. Now, if our whole lives are based on one giant misperception, then by definition, all the other perceptions we have made throughout our lives must be false. Imagine that! We really are living a lie because we are *making things up in our heads*. Thus, we distort the outcome of events in our lives based on our misperceptions—ones that stem from the beginning of time, and are perpetually revised based on our upbringing, our education, our laws, our country of origin, our religion, our cultural bias and our individual personalities as well. Goodness! It is a wonder that any of us can really understand each other. "All in the world is a little queer, except me and thee, and even thee is a little queer."

If we understand the notion of separation and all the misperceptions that spring from that, we can look at our lives. We can unravel the clutter and confusion. Our feelings of lack and disconnection stem from being in the Ego Mind instead of the Right Mind. Once you begin to really see what is happening here on earth and why, you will no longer have this great void of feeling separate and isolated from your true inner essence. In a practical sense, this means that **every time you feel disconnected, out of sync with your natural birthright of love, peace and inner joy, you have to look at what you are perceiving and correct the error**. It means that you simply have to change your perceptions about a situation, an event or a person.

This may sound easier said than done. Let me give you a practical example. Say you are feeling anger or hatred toward someone who "did" something to you. Now, this anger and hatred do not make you feel any better, nor do they correct the damage done—all these feelings do is keep you in that disconnected place, the place lacking in love. But you can re-examine the situation from the perspective that *we are all one* — and God loves us all equally. Our spirits are merely separated by a body, and we project our own deep feelings of guilt onto others. But projecting does not help us—it is itself a misperception. If we stop doing that, we can release our anger, and let go of our bitterness and resentment in such a way that we can actually feel love for that person. When we feel this love, we are truly reconnecting with our inner essence—our true, uninjured spirit.

When we project our guilt onto others we do so from the Ego Mind. It is not possible to do it from the Right Mind. We must understand that the Ego Mind is man-made, and consists of anything that is the *opposite of love*. Love is the essence of our true self. Any negativity, fear, doubt, judgment, criticism, guilt, shame or anger comes from our Ego Mind, the mind that has "separated" from God. Because of our guilt the Ego Mind keeps us in fear. Part of its job is to keep us from *reconnecting to spirit*. Essentially, the job of the Ego Mind is to destroy our link to God and our true essence, which is one of love. It does a good job of keeping us separated from our inner essence.

Having accepted the rules of the game before we come to earth, we take on individual bodies and hence we can no longer "see" ourselves as being all connected. This is a big part of our confusion. We think we are bodies. When we "see" another person as "separate" from us, that is separate from God, (we are all extensions of God), then we "attack" them, we project our guilt onto them. We also do this when we start to defend our positions once we are attacked. If we could look past the body and into their spirit, we would see ourselves as *mirror images* of each other and we would no longer want to harm them. It is often said that when we get angry with someone, it's because we are seeing something in them that we recognise as our own. Essentially, we are angry with ourselves. We can correct these errors of perception and find our way back to love.

The Ego Mind's job is to see "sin" in others, that *they* have done some evil or wrong to us, themselves or to others. Hence, we feel we have a right to be angry with them. The truth is that if we attack someone else, we are attacking God and our own selves. The only way past these problems is to change our perceptions about the person. We must simply forgive them and ourselves for our errors of perception. I will discuss this principle further in a later chapter, but for now let me give you an example from my own life of a time when I overcame misperception and created miracles for myself.

There was a period of time when I was feeling hard done by, by people at work. They all seemed to be out to get me. I was attracting bad behaviour non-stop. Once I understood the notion of "separation" and the Ego Mind, though, I was able to correct my error in thinking. I realised that by feeling "hard done by," I was assuming the role of the victim. But since my natural state really is one of love and peace, I was able to actively forgive each person and situation that was troubling me. I released all the negative energy that was bonding me to that situation. I freed myself of the Ego Mind's cycle of negativity, guilt and projection and was able to move on—back into my *true* state of peace and connection. I didn't have to ask anyone else to change their behaviour, you see—I simply shifted my own perception and the problem was solved.

Our lives can truly be miraculous. There is no need to be caught in a cycle of guilt, hard feelings, and isolation. That is the *opposite* of our natural state. Our only purpose, as spiritual beings on this planet, is to overcome the notion of separation—which was not even true in the first instance. All of our fears, doubts and judgments and negativity stem from this false premise. All we need to do to come back to our true essence, the love within us, is to reconnect with our inner essence. Once we do this, we will automatically see the beauty within others—we will see them as we see ourselves. From there, our lives can become miraculous. As *A Course in Miracles* states: "there is no order of difficulty in miracles." Miracles are simply changes in our perception; the big ones are just as great as the small ones.

In his book, *Power versus Force*, Dr David Hawkins talks about the levels of consciousness and how we, as spiritual beings, can move up the scale of enlightenment. To do this, we must move to a position of power. How do we do this? The only true power comes from surrendering our personal agenda. That means, we must let go of the agenda of the Ego Mind, and tap into the Higher Self (or Right Mind). Only then can we access our true potential, our true power.

Dr Hawkins has calibrated a system for measuring how spiritually powerful people are. According to his system, the majority of people on the planet are operating at a spiritual level of 200. At this level, people are living in a place of shame, guilt, apathy, fear, anxiety, desire, anger, and pride. Essentially, these are all traits of the Ego Mind. In order to move out of the Ego Mind—to become more spiritual and hence more powerful—we need to shift into more positive modes of operation, i.e. *love*. *A Course in Miracles* tells us that we can do this by changing our perception and offering forgiveness to others and ourselves. In effect, Dr Hawkins research validates what *ACIM* states, but gives us a practical way to do this.

With an acceptance and an understanding of our true spiritual life purpose—to overcome the misperception of separation from spirit, and why have such deep feelings of guilt—we can find a way forward to reconnect with our inner essence, the love within. We now have a guided path to move forward in our lives. Having a spiritual life purpose gives us a real sense of belonging, security—a place we can call home. That's why this is Step 1 of the 5 steps to living the life you deserve—it's your foundation. Our true home is a place of love and connection—connection to others, connection to spirit. Once we have this firmly in place, Step 2 will emerge naturally.

Now, how can you know that you have truly made a reconnection with your inner self, your Higher Self? Well, you will tell yourself! Your Higher Self will speak to you through your senses— visual, kinesthetic or auditory. You may have conversations with your Higher Self, or it may communicate with you via someone else or some sign. For example, I may be seeking an answer to some specific thing that is bothering me. I may meet someone in the supermarket who just happens to drop some information that is relevant to my question. Or I may see a book with a headline that jumps out at me. If I see or hear something *more than once*, I know that's the answer I've been looking for.

It's about cultivating your ability to pay attention to these signs and communications. You may find it is taking you awhile to pick up on any messages. Personally, I use Angel Cards if I have a specific question. Sometimes, I don't get the answer I'm looking for, but it's still something I needed to know. I've found that bad results have come when I've chosen to ignore something the cards told me. I am unable to make a decision now without consulting my Angel Cards—and that really helps me. Because I have a very strong communication with my Higher Self, I know, and she knows, that this is the way to get through to me if I have been missing her conversations or other signs.

Connecting with your Higher Self on a daily basis will take some practice. You will become more sensitive to his/her modes of communication as time goes by. In the chapter on daily techniques, I'll show you some practices that will help you to fine tune your senses. Hooking into your Higher Self is an important result of building your spiritual foundation, and it will save you enormous time in the long run. More and more, you will no longer get led down the wrong path or make the wrong decisions and waste precious time.

The next step, Step 2, is finding your Life Path as a human and finding clarity within that meaningful life purpose. In this step, you will also be focused on identifying that meaningful purpose (or career), - now that you have identified your spiritual foundation. From this foundation, you'll clarify your identity, giving you clearer focus and direction in your life. It makes it easier to live a more rich and meaningful life, on path and on purpose. I will outline a way to discover that path, which is a path to wealth and happiness, but also a path to our true and meaningful career, life direction, or purpose. It clarifies who we are and what we are like, and thereby finding a place where we can do the most good, make the most money, and make a contribution all at the same time.

The key to Step 2 is to find out what your natural talents are and to be doing *that which you do easily*. Doing what you are good at is a way of choosing ease instead of struggle. If something is hard, it means you shouldn't be doing it. Maybe you need help from others who have those particular skills. No shame in that at all! When you are in flow, the other people and resources that you need will *turn up naturally*. If what you are doing feels too hard, it means you are out of flow. Chapters 4 and 5 will outline this step in more detail, but first let me say a word about guilt and lack.

Now, I know that when something goes wrong for me—such as when I'm out of flow and doing something I shouldn't be doing—I get this huge sense of guilt and start punishing myself. You may very well have felt this too. This guilt, this feeling of lack and deprivation, does not come because you are a failure. You may be attempting to do something that is out of line with your natural talents. You may need to pass the task on to someone else. The self-punishing feeling *is not your natural state*. You feel that way because of the separation from God I have been talking about—the separation from your true self or Higher Consciousness.

The Ego Mind has created anger and self-blame as a way to keep us separate from our inner selves. As soon as we get angry, we leave our reasonable, rational Right Mind and go into the *wrong mind*. We start to judge other people. We try to justify how we are right and they have "sinned" against others or us. We call for punishment. We project this guilt—really caused by our guilt from our separation— onto other people. Perhaps they have made a mistake or erred. But maintaining our anger against them only keeps you trapped in the circle of negativity. This is just what the Ego Mind wants you to do. Maintaining any negativity in your body, mind or aura keeps *you* trapped, *not* the other person.

It keeps you from reconnecting with your inner self. It keeps you separated, separated from your natural birthright of inner peace, happiness and joy. So, in order to reconnect you need to clear yourself of this trapped negativity. We will look at this in a later chapter so that you can live the life you deserve.

As you begin this work of building your spiritual foundation, you may find it is hard to know where to begin. If you are having trouble finding a way to spiritual reconnection, there are some simple things you can do to get started. Here are just a few that I did for myself and they all, in their own way, helped me back to love.

Join a group that sparks your interest. This is a wonderful way to increase connection with others and yourself at the same time. It can help to feel that you are making a meaningful contribution on this planet. For example, I joined a theatre group and got involved in doing things I genuinely love: dancing and singing. In this way I was able to awaken my spark inside and felt better about myself. It helped me to remember my true identity as well, to reconnect with my own natural state of joy.

You may also consider joining a church group. I am not religious at all. However, this was one of the main avenues for me to witness love, support and nurturing firsthand. The people in my church group made me feel welcome and gave me a sense of belonging. In this way, I was gradually able to repair my sense of separation and reconnect with spirit.

It can be helpful to make a contribution to others as well. I joined the Red Cross Telecross Volunteer Group. In that program, volunteers telephone an elderly person to see how they doing and if they need anything. Steps are in place if they do not respond to the call. This can sometimes be the highlight of someone's day! So, I had the benefit of feeling good about myself for being able to contribute to someone else's life. In turn, the person on the other end of the phone knew that someone cared about them.

These are just a few of the things that you might consider doing. And remember, anything you choose is a step in the right direction! Baby steps are fine when you are walking towards reconnection to self— back to love.

The Path of Least Resistance

"It is as important to figure out what you're not going to do as it is to know what you are going to do."
— **Michael Dell**

Step 2: Discovering your Framework - identity
Part I: How to find your Human Life Path, your Purpose, and your Flow

In these next two chapters, we will be looking at **Step 2 of the five steps to living the life you deserve**. I call this step "discovering your framework" and it is, essentially, a two-part process. First, you need to discover your Life Path. Then, *from* your Life Path, you will discover your human life purpose, or purposes—as you may have several. Your human life purposes stem naturally from your Life Path. I will discuss those—along with your *natural talents base* — in more detail in the next chapter.

What's important to understand is this: discovering your Life Path will give you a clearer *direction* to your natural talents base and, hence, your life purposes. When you are operating from this place, your life flows more easily. You will feel a strong sense of connection with your true self. Hence, uncovering your Life Path will allow you to find your way back to your true self, your spirit.

Once you are in communication again with your spirit, from here you can choose a life purpose— or purposes—that *will be based on your natural talents* and thus, generate the most abundance. You will feel validated. Step 2 helps you gain your human identity, and when you are in flow, you will *know* you have re-connected to your inner essence, your spirit.

In this chapter, I'll focus on the first aspect of Step 2— discovering your Life Path and life purposes, easily and effortlessly. Once you find your Life Path, your life purpose/s will emerge *naturally* from that path. This is about finding your *true human identity*. Your purpose/s will become so obvious that you will wonder how and why you've struggled with this your whole life! It will become *clear* to you what type of work will be most satisfying and absorbing—as well as emotionally, mentally and financially *rewarding*. This is what I mean by "true wealth," and it emerges as a result of identifying your Life Path. From here, you will begin to act from *within your natural talents* — the talents you were born with. When you are acting from this place, you maximise both your ability to give back meaningfully to the planet as well as to reap your own inner and outer rewards.

How do you know when you are on the right Life Path? You will have a clear sense of direction. You will feel *validated*, as all of those little talents and skills—the ones you didn't think you could really transfer into wealth—will be drawn out. What will you end up with? A very useable basketful of sellable skills! You will no longer be embarrassed to claim your natural talents, or to tell others about them. You will finally feel recognised for *who you really are*.

Throughout life we learn lots of skills, usual ones to do with daily living, health, safety, security and the like. When you start a career, you do specific jobs. You learn the specific skills required for that job. Sometimes those skills become so ingrained that we *lose our identity* to them. For example, if I have worked as an accountant, a teacher or an engineer, when someone asks me what I do, I say: "I am a teacher...I am an accountant...I am an engineer." We tend to explain who we are by what we do, rather than saying "I am a human being and I perform accounting work." We define ourselves by our work, rather than *who we are*.

The problem with this approach is precisely this: *we lose our identity to our learned skills*. At the same time, we become totally confused about *who* we really are. We become removed from our *real* talents and *natural* skills. Often, we're not sure whether we even *like* doing what we do.

How do you know you are on the wrong Life Path? It will show up in a variety of ways, which all amount to a *lack of love*. These include: high levels of stress, low energy levels, and over-use of addictive substances such as coffee, sugar or alcohol. You begin to need all sorts of therapies to overcome physical or emotional pain. You long for the weekend, because you don't really enjoy what you're doing during the week. You begin to look older than your years. Your sleep patterns become erratic. In a word, you *lose joy* in your life.

Unfortunately, most of these behaviours are typical for the vast majority of working people. I recently saw a study indicating that 87% of employed people were looking for a new job at the beginning of 2012. This is another sign that *all is not well*. People often get into a pattern of changing jobs, thinking that the next one will be better. Quite often, changing jobs doesn't really improve matters because what's happening *inside* comes right along with you. Taking a holiday is only a temporary fix. More often, what we really need to do is stop and take stock of *what* we are doing and *why*. Yet, people rarely feel that this is an option because the monetary aspect is frightening—we're afraid of losing income.

How often have you heard that you should "do what you love"? In reality, all too often we *don't know what that is*. Figuring out your Life Path will clarify this question. Another thing someone might say is, "Well, I love sitting watching television." So the question becomes, "How do I make a living out of sitting around watching television?" How can I pay the bills by doing this? The underlying point is this: If you are doing *meaningful, relevant* work emerging from your true Life Path, you will have no need to use television as an escape. Now, watching television could be a form of relaxation—but it would not be your only form of enjoyment. The true enjoyment—indeed, the *joy*—of life comes from making a contribution to the world by doing what *you were meant to do*.

This is the stumbling block for most people: "How can I make any money doing what I love?" Often, we may have dug ourselves into a financial hole with a large mortgage, credit card debts or other loans. This creates a financial noose around our necks. We feel trapped, unable to make a life change because we depend upon a certain income. So, the biggest trap we get stuck in is the financial trap. But what is really underneath that? The real trap is *fear*. Fear of the unknown. Fear of failure. Fear of embarking on something new.

Now, what if some of the things you loved doing *and* do well were also *recognisable skills* that you could develop into something meaningful? What if you could earn a living from them? As I said, the financial trap keeps the vast majority of us from recognising our true natural talents; this, in turn, keeps us from our true Life Path. This is the biggest barrier standing in the way of finding your *true identity*. Doing work that is not fulfilling to your true nature is soul destroying. It accelerates the loss of joy in your life. Your purpose becomes simply to *get by*, to merely survive, or to pay the bills. Your *spirit is dulled*, thus making it harder to connect with your human life purpose—what *you are meant to do*. This makes it impossible to re-connect with your spiritual life purpose, to connect back with love.

How will I know I am on the right Life Path? Choosing a Life Path gives you instant direction and a narrower road to focus on. This may not sound like much fun, but believe me it is *big* fun! Once you have identified your Life Path, you will have a clear sense of who you *really* are—what things you can do easily and naturally, and what things you cannot. The beauty of this is that you'll be able to see which tasks others should be doing for you instead. Your true nature and natural skill set will *match* the Path you are on and everything will become easier for you. You will begin to feel that you *finally* understand who you are. You will regain your joie de vivre. You will feel like a huge weight has been lifted from your shoulders. Your work will feel easy *and* be fun to do. No effort is required. Your attractiveness will increase and people will want to join with you. Your life will feel like it is in flow.

The key here is precisely the idea of *flow*. If something *feels hard* to do—this means you should not be doing it. That feeling of "this is hard" comes when you are acting *outside of your natural skill set*, and at this point you should get someone else to do it. Similarly, from a spiritual point of view, if you are feeling anxious or are not attracting what you want, it means you are temporarily *out of sync* with the universe. You need to clear yourself, change your perceptions, or simply wait until the disruption passes.

Do you have to wait and just accidentally stumble upon your Life Path? **Is there a quick way to discover your true identity and hence your true Life Path and life purpose?** Yes! There is. That's the point of this chapter. Sometimes in life, we may be lucky enough to just stumble onto the right path. That is precisely what happened with me when I was making my movie. And within that path, my purpose was very clear. It felt *right*, fun and joyful because all of my natural talents came to the fore. Resources appeared when I needed them *without a lot of struggle* on my part. Now, at that stage, I wondered how I could make a living out of that path and earn reasonable dollars in the immediate short term. Like many people, I could not convince myself that this was possible. It seemed like a luxury and not a real career move. So, what did I do? I did what so many others have done and *gave up that path and that purpose*. I continued down the path of a profession of learned skills. I continued to do accounting work. The fortunate thing for most of us is that your Higher Self will *bring you other opportunities* if you do not capitalise on the first opportunity.

A big part of my decision to go back on the wrong path—the path of learned skills, i.e. accounting— was that I hadn't *realised* I was on the right Life Path at the time. It had happened naturally and effortlessly, so it wasn't as clear to me that I was straying from the *right* path. As I continued my personal journey of self-discovery, however, I came across an incredibly useful tool. This tool helped me to put the pieces back together, to understand that when I was making my movie *I was on the right Life Path*. It showed me aspects of my true identity that explained why making my movie had felt so right, whereas my career in accounting often felt so wrong. This tool is the *shortcut* that I would like to show you, here, to discovering your true Life Path and life purpose's.

The Wealth Dynamics Profiling System, developed by Roger Hamilton, is based on the ancient Chinese philosophy of the I Ching. This system outlines how you can obtain and maintain wealth — *both inner and outer wealth* —if you choose to follow your true Life Path. Your Life Path indicates natural talents and skill sets that *you were born with*. Once you have chosen to follow your correct Life Path, your life purpose will *emerge* as it will be related to your Life Path. When you are in your correct Life Path, you will feel that your life is in flow. You will *attract* all of the resources, people, money and ideas that you need.

From a spiritual perspective, being on the right Human Life Path automatically helps you feel more connected to your inner self. However, I have found that you will still need to do the work required to stay connected to your spirit, your Higher Self. Later in the book, I will give you some clear strategies and techniques for maintaining connection with your Higher Self—which will help you immeasurably to *stay* on the right Life Path. Wealth Dynamics is about *finding* your Life Path in the first place, and it shows you the path of least resistance to *your* best means of wealth creation.

Roger Hamilton's system divides the various life paths and means of creating wealth into eight profiles. For each profile, Roger provides real-life examples to help you identify the tactics that each of these successful people has used to carve out their niche and create wealth. Essentially, these high-profile individuals *discovered* the talents that they were born with and *capitalised* on these talents to carve out a successful career. According to Roger, they followed the path of 'least resistance,"—they did what they loved and what they were good at. It may not have been immediate, but they stuck to their chosen field and worked through various positions until they found their exact niche, the path that created the greatest wealth.

Wealth Dynamics outlines eight life paths that people can choose from. Considering the large number and variety of occupations that one could perform, this may not sound like a large number. But within each Life Path, there are a variety of corollary skills and talents you may also possess; these *supplement* your main skill set.

To hear Roger Hamilton explain his system in greater depth, you can visit the Free Bonuses section of the website listed on the front of this book. In the meantime, I'll give you a brief overview of the eight life paths identified in the Wealth Dynamics system.

1. the CREATOR - is good at creating profitable businesses, but should not manage anyone or anything
2. the STAR - relies on their personality and has an obligation to deliver; they are their own brand and their brand is their business
3. the SUPPORTER - are great networkers; and they should either run a business or manage businesses
4. the DEAL MAKER - relies on relationships and reacting intuitively when the best opportunities arise; they love putting people and deals together
5. the TRADER - someone who hunts out bargains
6. the ACCUMULATOR - grows assets incrementally and sticks to a successful system
7. LORD - likes to control the cash
8. the MECHANIC - they like to fine-tune systems to make a better mousetrap, for example; they should not create systems, only fine-tune them.

According to Roger Hamilton, this is a *wealth profiling system*. It enables you to identify *your* path of least resistance. It gives you a "wealth creation profile" that suits your personal strengths. Each of the eight profiles includes its own unique strategy for creating wealth. As you will see, it is a proven path that many successful people have followed. Here are just a few of the things that the Wealth Dynamics system can provide you:

- A method for you to focus your time investment

- A route to clarity and certainty of your Path
- A permanent foundation
- A way to distinguish your wealth creation process in the industry or profession that you are currently in
- A method to select the right role models
- A tool to gain clearer understanding of yourself
- A reference point for your learning and growth

The Wealth Dynamics system is a perfect way to begin **discovering your framework**. It allows you to identify your best Life Path—the one that will allow you to make a meaningful life from the talents that you *naturally* possess. With this system as part of your framework, you'll have a solid basis for choosing life purposes that will increase your wealth and your ability to contribute to the world. According to Roger Hamilton, there are two questions that each of us needs to ask:

1. Which path to wealth suits our natural character and personality best?
2. Once we know which path to wealth is best for us, what are the steps we should take, and what are the rules for that particular wealth creation game?

Now, as I've mentioned before, when I created and executed my movie I was in total *flow*. Things came to me easily and effortlessly. If there were any obstacles I thought of a way over, around, or through them. Doing what I *was* good at — utilising my natural talents and choosing the right team to do what *they* did best — made this experience the biggest fun one could have! When you connect with the right Life Path, you shortcut your connection to your Higher Self. You will feel different. Everything will become *easier*.

To give you a practical look at what this system is all about, we can use my friend, Celine Healy's personal profile. Throughout this chapter I will use personal pronouns interchangeably, as if the name : Celine and I are synonymous It illustrates where *I* need to be in order to create my greatest wealth. As I said before, when I speak about wealth I mean *both inner and outer wealth*.

Name: Celine Healy			
WEALTH DYNAMICS PROFILE Wealth Frequencies			
Dynamo: 56%	Blaze: 36%	Tempo: 8%	Steel: 0%
Primary Wealth Profile: Star			

[Radar chart showing eight profiles around the octagon: Mechanic, Creator, Star, Supporter, Deal maker, Trader, Accumulator, Lord. Axes labeled Dynamo (top), Blaze (right), Tempo (bottom), Steel (left). Additional labels: Intuitive, Sensory, Introvert, Extrovert.]

As you can see from my/Celine's results, my personal path of least resistance to wealth creation is in The Star Profile. My secondary natural skill base falls in The Creator category, and I have some Supporter and Mechanic skills. I know my nature has two extremes: I am highly visionary, inspirational, and creative—very abstract skills. But I also have a practical aspect to these skills, which is why I outline steps in point order when I need to write out something for someone else to follow. This is my way of making myself clear. This part of my skill set can be seen in The Mechanic aspect of my profile. I believe it has been deeply ingrained due to the number of years I spent doing accounting work.

Now, let's look at The Star Profile in order to see what type of work or career would most suit me. You can see that the diagram indicates that The Star section goes right to the end of the border. It's important to remember that when I took the quiz I was doing accounting work and had done so for many years. Now, accountants need to be on the other side of the line. That's where you would find their natural skill set, perhaps as a Lord, an Accumulator or as a Mechanic. You can see from the diagram that I barely have any natural skills in those areas. This means that I spent years trying to fit into a slot that was foreign to my nature and natural skill set.

The diagram indicates that I *should* spend the majority of my time in the Star Profile—and that means being out front, creating and magnifying my brand. I should be leading, giving talks, being the brand either for my own business or someone else's. Essentially, I should be inspiring and motivating people. Now, all those years I was working in accounting, i.e. actually doing the accounting work, I wasn't able to do any of those things. It was only when I did peripheral networking tasks that I was able to utilise some of those natural talents.

What was the result? I constantly felt restless, as though I did not fit in. I tried to make the job into something else by developing business networks and giving talks to groups of business people, but it wasn't quite right. I was constantly stressed out; consequently, I tried all kinds of different therapies to overcome the physical and emotional pain in my body. I went into addictive behaviour. I tried to drown my spirit with alcohol because I could not see my way out. I believe my Higher Self would break through at times and give me the message that I was on the wrong path. At one point, I retrained as a Stress Counselor—which was a step along the right path. However, it was financially impossible to survive in the short term because of all the bills and mortgages I had entrapped myself with. You see, being an accountant also paid well in the monetary sense. So I was in the financial trap that I talked about earlier. Working as a Stress Counselor was a financial dead end initially as the set up time to build a successful practice took much longer than originally anticipated—and I was right back to accounting.

However, whenever I went back to detail-oriented work, I was unable to last for longer than three months at a time. I kept making mistakes and feeling stressed out all the time. Ultimately, I had to make a permanent change of direction.

I decided to try sales. At first, it was challenging because I had no sales experience. However, I *creatively* sought the services of a professional resume writer who was able to write my CV based on skill sets, qualities and values rather than experience. This enabled me to launch into sales—which was on the right path. But since I had no real deep connection to sales per se, I was still fulfilling the wrong *purpose*. You see, what I was really good at was inspiring and motivating people. I needed to find a way to do that! Hence, my new and *true* Life Path and life purposes—which I will outline in the next chapter.

So, you might ask, "How can I find my Life Path when I do not want to be in business? I just want to have a career or a job in the industry that I am already in." According to Roger Hamilton, your Wealth Profile *does not* dictate your industry, but it can guide you to *your most appropriate role* within that industry. Let's take the property industry, for example:

Profiles v Industries

Example of multiple Profiles within the same Industry

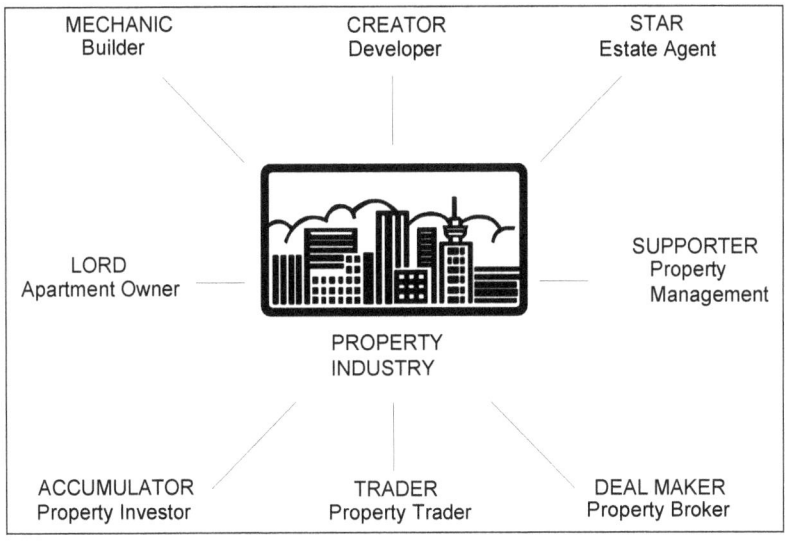

As you can see from this, within a particular industry you may have one clear role to play—one that suits your natural talents. Your life does leave clues. The times in my life when things were the *easiest* were: when I was lecturing or tutoring, when I set up networks, when I gave inspiring speeches at functions, when I motivated individuals or helped them to find their life purpose, when I directed my movie and when I inspired the best people in Australia to work on my movie for free. These are all *natural* Star Profile attributes.

These successes—all related to the gift of the gab—were so easy for me. In a way, that's the confusing part! They did not *seem like skills*—so I never noticed them as real skills. Hence, a lot of my work life, probably 80% or more, was spent in doing work that did not utilise my natural talents. This led to stress and burn out quite frequently. I also discovered that the majority of people are operating *outside* of their natural skill set—which is why so many of us are stressed out! Another thing I've observed is that, due to the lack of structure, purpose and direction in many people's lives, they are not living confident and meaningful lives. So many of us are just "hanging in there." Believe me, I remember what that felt like.

When I did the Wealth Dynamics profiling test, so much of this became clear to me. My overriding talents are in the Star Profile; but I had spent the majority of my life doing accounting work. I was using only learned skills and was operating totally outside of my profile. Hence, I found everything *difficult* and became stressed and burnt out easily.

When you find out you have been working in the wrong profile for most of your life, it comes as a shock. You start to wonder how you can possibly make any money in this new profile—which was my next dilemma.

There is an interesting saying: "The luckier I get, the more I attract." When you are in flow, your attraction factor increases exponentially. You leave the path of the hard struggle and move to one of ease. That's why Roger Hamilton describes the Wealth Dynamics Profiling System as a way to show you the *path of least resistance*. This system helps people do what they *love* in a career or business sense. Once you have identified *your* path of least resistance, you will find yourself on the right Life Path. From here, you will find your true purpose.

For most people, it is a difficult moment when they find out what their true profile is. When, like myself, you are used to thinking of yourself in terms of your "learned skills," the profile can create a great deal of uncertainty. This is because those "learned skills" can hide your *true* nature, your true talents. This can make it very difficult to recognise what your true talents are, especially if you haven't been using them for a long time. There may be a long period of self-discovery ahead.

Now, you can take the shortcut by *no longer doing what you are not good at* and switching to doing what you are good at. Yes, it takes time and it takes courage to choose your right Life Path. However, the *lifelong rewards* are there for the taking. Once you understand yourself better, you will ultimately find your Life Path much *easier* than what you have been doing previously. It may take a leap of faith. There may be a period of transition. But, believe me, it is worth it.

How do I know? Because I have been lucky enough to see this and to change my life for the better. At first, it was a shock to see that my profile was so far from what I had been doing my whole life. In essence, as a Star Profile, I am my own business product. The greatest contribution I can make is by leading from the front and inspiring others. This is what I'm good at. My moment of wealth creation comes from defining and re-defining my identity and then delivering that. I need to be the brand of my own business or the brand representing someone else's business; I need to constantly use my natural skills of improvisation and adaptation, refining my brand to suit the situation. It's a bit like Madonna, creating a new look every few years. If I do not do this, then I fail to capitalise on my strengths and I can disappear into the crowd. You see, each profile has a moment of wealth creation. If you fail to capitalise on it then you're not maximising your position within your Life Path.

The Wealth Dynamics profiling system gave me a *direction*, but I still needed to clarify what my actual talents were. I needed to know more about myself and how I operate in the world, so that I could fine-tune my steps towards wealth creation. In the next chapter, I will tell you about just such a system! Together, these two profiling systems gave me the knowledge that I needed to understand myself. With this flood of self-knowledge, I was able to finally choose the right Human Life Path for me and get back into flow. It really is all about finding *your* true identity.

You see, someone else's strategies will most likely conflict with yours. They will work for them. You need to find *your own* life path. Your life path will match your personality best. Your life path will work for you because of *who you are*, your particular identity, and not because of *what you do*. Knowing your own individual identity within that life path will put you in flow.

The Wealth Dynamics system *defines* this flow for you, outlines what strategies *you* need to take, and defines a specific critical path to wealth creation, for you. As I said earlier, it is about matching who you are first, and then finding out what you should be doing. Most people are operating from the 'wrong' path. I know from personal experience, as I did that for many years. I had my greatest moments of success when I was, by *accident*, on the right Life Path. I lost great amounts of money and wealth attributes when I was in the *wrong* profile—I was playing the wrong game.

Now, in order to clarify what your Wealth Dynamics profile can show you, I'll talk a bit more about my own profile here. Looking at my Star Profile, we can see the steps that *I need* to take in order to be successful and to achieve my greatest wealth.

My results indicate that the majority of my time should be spent in the Dynamo and Blaze sides of the diagram. In the Dynamo aspect, the attributes indicate that I am: energised, dynamic, creative, great at getting things started but terrible at getting things finished. How true that has been for me! Whereas, in the Blaze aspect, I am: passionate, outgoing, great at networking and meeting new people, but am easily distracted from the task at hand. Yes. Another problem area for me. I am like a butterfly that has flitted from one bright shiny object to another. I felt each new opportunity offered a better outcome! Oh, how wrong can one person be, but continually!

So, the Wealth Dynamics Profiling System offers us *steps to achieve our greatest wealth opportunities*. Within our individual profile, our secondary profiles will influence how we create and leverage these wealth opportunities. As you commit to your own profile area, you operate from a narrower base, i.e. your niche talents, and you, will gradually build your skills to mastery. At this point, you will feel the effects of *flow*. When you are in flow you will attract opportunities; you will genuinely enjoy what you are doing. This is the place you might describe as "loving what you do and doing what you love." Now, it doesn't happen immediately. Like all things in life that are worth having, it takes a bit of time. It takes effort to build upon your natural skills. But, I promise you, if you continue to operate within your correct Life Path, your financial wealth will automatically follow.

So, my Star Profile indicates that I need to clearly define what value I can contribute to others. I have to create a unique identity and continue to refine that identity. All stars who are truly successful continue to do that. Within this profile, I need to be able to know clearly who and what I am and stand for such that when others talk about me, based on my branding strategy, I will have a good idea of what they would be saying.

How I create my own value is by building exposure, crystallising my brand and fine- tuning my talents. I need to have a team around me who can help me with creating ownership of my product and myself; I am, in essence, my own product. I can add value to others by promoting their products and services or by creating my own unique products and services. I do that in concert with my team, which would include Creators and Mechanics. I also need Dealmakers who can seek out and promote me or my products, as well as align with others who can open doors for me. My Supporter will help negotiate my fees and commissions, the financial aspects of maximising my wealth.

Stars can get in their own way. They can get carried away, burn out easily and self- destruct. Because they are so intuitive, they are constantly thinking of new ways to brand themselves and create new products. Their most productive use of time is to use their creativity; however, they need the *correct team* around them in order to maximise this time of creation. They should be doing things that are fun for them; however, they still need to refine their output to deliver the greatest monetary or exposure value. They must ask themselves, "What is it about this product or service that is different from others and will create my own little niche?" Then, in order to maximise wealth creation, they need a good team to market their product or service.

As you can see, there are specific steps within the Wealth Dynamics Profiling System that will help you to identify your strengths and weaknesses. Once you begin to see some of the natural talents you were born with, you'll have a much better idea about where you're heading and your life purposes will begin to pop up automatically.

The important thing to take from all of this? *If you are operating outside your profile you will not create lasting success or wealth.* If you operate *within* your profile, and follow ALL of the five steps to living the life you deserve, you *will* reconnect with your inner self. You will vibrate a particular energy. You will start to attract the people, resources, and money that you need. You will be in *resonance*. Being in resonance is a clear sign that you are on the right Path. It happens when you are aligned with your Life Path; it happens easily and effortlessly. To shortcut your way to the right Life Path, the Wealth Dynamics Profiling System is an excellent place to start!

There's Nobody Like You

"Getting the right people in the right jobs is a lot more important than developing a strategy".
– Jack Welsh

Step 2: Discovering your Framework- Identity
Part II: Identify and Implement your Natural Base Talents - Reconnect with Your Passions

In this chapter I will look at a proven method toward helping you discover your *natural base talents*. This is the ideal extension of discovering your Life Path. With it, we'll work on the second aspect of **building your framework**—discovering and claiming your natural, God-given talents and using them to achieve your life purposes.

When you are operating from your natural talents base your life flows more easily. Your *Life Path gives you a clear direction to your natural talents base* and you will actually feel as though you have made a connection with your true self. It is a way back to finding true self, your spirit. Once you have identified your Life Path you can then choose a life purpose/s that will maximise your ability to generate abundance because you will be using your natural talents. You will feel validated. Step 2 helps you gain your human identity, and when you are in flow, you will "know" you have reconnected to your inner essence, your spirit.

This aspect of my journey arose when, having identified my Life Path, I was unclear about how I should go about adapting to that life path. I had been off track for some time and I felt an imperative to shortcut my road to success. This is one of my natural modes of operation, one that I instinctively use in order to create meaning in my life. Now, I want to share my *shortcut* with you to get you more quickly on the road to success!

In this chapter we look at the Kolbe A™ Index to fine-tune what your natural talents are, to celebrate these talents and learn how to use these to your *best* advantage! Having read the background and history of the Kolbe A Index myself, I feel it is my duty to simplify this information for you. If you are someone who enjoys all the finer details, this information is easily accessible via any Google search. For now, let's look briefly at what the Kolbe A Index measures.

Research indicates that there are three aspects of the mind: the knowing, the feeling, and the willing. In her system, Kathy Kolbe defines these as *thinking, feeling,* and *doing*. In the past, research has tended to focus on the parts that were more easily measurable—the thinking and the feeling. Kathy Kolbe, faced with enormous adversity in her life, knew instinctively that in order to overcome these difficulties, she needed to call upon her deep-rooted instincts. She needed to concentrate on the *doing* aspects of her nature.

Kolbe discovered the notion of "conation," which had been long-overlooked due to the difficulty in measuring it. She describes conation as "the faculty of the brain that drives you to take purposeful action according to your instincts. Conative abilities are the natural, inherent, and unchanging talents that, when acted on, lead to success and well-being as you use your creative energy to solve problems."

To me, conative abilities are the ways in which you *instinctively react to situations*. In that moment of reaction, you use your natural, God-given talents to move towards the best solution that *you* can see. When you do this, you operate from a position of creativity, a position of *power* and boundless energy. This is a wonderful tool to clarify who you really are and how you operate within your Life Path. Having discovered and chosen your Life Path, you have *gained* direction. Now, you can now gain *focus* within that direction by implementing your *natural abilities* rather than just your learned skills, as I mentioned earlier. The truth is, learned skills can *mask* who you really are, hindering your progress toward self- discovery and mastery over your life.

The Kolbe A Index measures *your natural way of doing*, the way you act instinctively. It identifies your natural strengths. Using Wealth Dynamics, I was slotted into a general category: The Star Profile—which helped me to identify my Life Path. With the Kolbe A Index, I am able to *refine* who I am within that general category. In order to have the greatest possible definition in your life to build a solid framework, it's imperative that you try both systems. *Using the Kolbe A Index will help you to clearly define and refine your life purpose/s within your Life Path.* The Kolbe A Index results are so individualised that only 5% of the population is likely to have one just like yours. Wow! Only 5%! That makes me/you very special—very unique! Discovering and fine-tuning *who you are* in this specific, individualised way gives you a powerful resource to define your life purpose.

One of the remarkable results of taking the Kolbe A Index was the feeling that *someone knew who I was*. I felt recognised. It was a *validation* of who I was. What an incredible feeling! The Index described me to myself. It gave me permission to live and act precisely *from the place that feels most natural to me*. Not only that, it showed me several modes of operation that I feel comfortable within, and how I can best use them to achieve the maximum results!

So, here's how Wealth Dynamics and the Kolbe A Index work together: Wealth Dynamics allows you to figure out the big picture-your Life Path, the one *you are meant to be on*. Once you have established that, you need to understand your *natural, unique* talents so that you can start using them. Only by using your natural, instinctive, God-given talents can you create true wealth in your life and maximise your value. This is where the Kolbe A Index comes in; it will *show you* your natural talents. For example, how *I* operate best from within my instinctive abilities is by simplifying. That is what I am doing now, for you. By using the Kolbe A Index, you *will shortcut* your way to *immeasurable* success—true wealth, both inner and outer.

Kathy Kolbe's profiling system is divided into four distinct sections. First, the Fact Finder indicates how you *gather and share information*; Follow Thru is how you *arrange and design*. Quick Start reveals how you deal with *risks and uncertainty*. Finally, the Implementor section demonstrates how you handle *space and tangibles*.

When you see your Kolbe A Index results, you will have a powerful sense of being recognised. To give you an idea of how uncanny this can be, I'll share with you my first experience with Kathy Kolbe. I attended her lecture when she came to Australia and she called attention to my Index results for demonstration purposes. Now, at that time I didn't understand the results of my profile. When I looked at my results, I saw the profile of a failure with no definable skills to offer the world! You see, my Quick

Start score was 10—while in all the other categories the number was much lower. It didn't strike me as the most useful category to be in. However, Kathy's demonstration called the Glop Shop exercise revealed some interesting results.

First, she instructed me and the other two demonstration participants to step outside so that we couldn't hear what she was saying to the audience. Unbeknownst to us, she was predicting to the audience, based on our profiles, how *each of us would react* when given a specific task. When we came back in, Kathy instructed us to come up with an educational toy that would also be entertaining and instructional. She gave us three minutes to complete the task.

Well. What was I to do? I tried to discuss options with the other participants but they were so busy "doing" the task that they did not want to discuss what we would do. I see now that they were operating to a time limit rather than a beneficial outcome level. There were many distractions throughout the process, like the audience screaming to me that I was running out of time. All the while, my brain was working overtime to come up with a solution. I scanned the available objects on the table and I chose the brightest object that had the most potential for the outcome that I could perceive in that moment.

The outcome? I achieved the goal of the task in the shortest time possible because the demonstration created the circumstances in which *I operate best*. I operate to a deadline. I do not "do" things. I *think* about them and *create intuitively* what the best solution will be. It was such a hoot doing that demonstration! I went from thinking that my Kolbe A Index was the profile of a failure to seeing that it really indicated my *useable, natural talents*!

Throughout this chapter I will use personal pronouns synonymously to indicate that the words: Celine and I are interchangeable. So, let's look at my friend, Celine's personal Kolbe A Index results to see what natural talents I operate from, i.e. the instinctual methods that I consistently use to get results. My overall results show that I am terrific with future-oriented challenges and dealing with essential facts. I do not get bogged down with detailed information. If a project interests me, I say, "yes" even before I know the end of the question! Then I turn it into a productive adventure.

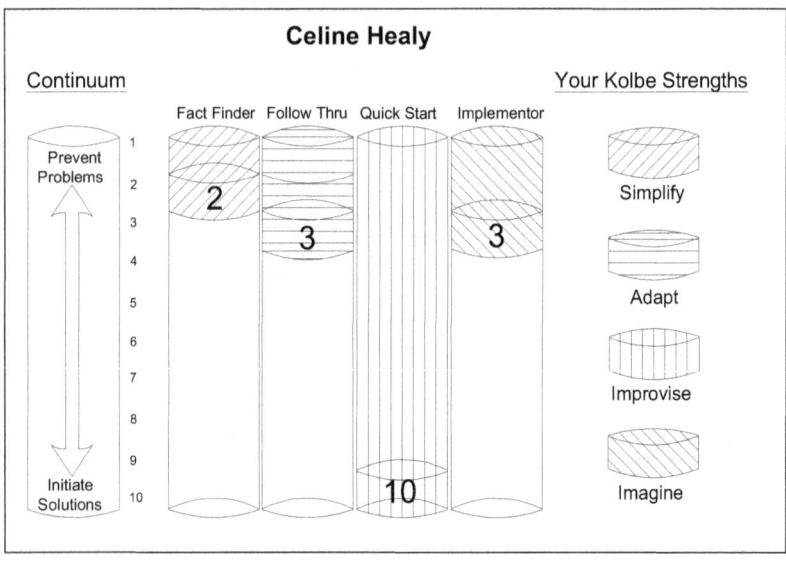

Looking at the four aspects defined above, let's take the Fact Finder category first. This indicates how I *gather and share information*: I simplify it. That's exactly what I'm doing with this book! I've brought together a lot of information and created a simple solution that you can easily apply to your own life for greater focus and meaning.

As for my Follow Thru, my ability to *arrange and design*, I have pretty much none! However, the Kolbe A Index suggests that I tend to adapt. I change the situation or data to suit myself rather than adapting my strategy to the structure. I generally tend to say to myself, "They don't really mean that, what they mean is this." Yes, I admit to that! This is one of the wonderful things about the Index—I feel validated for this part of my personality and I can see how it is useful, rather than feeling badly because I have a different style of Follow Thru than others.

Looking at my Quick Start aspect, how I deal with *risks and uncertainty* — you can see this is my highest number. That is because this is one of the conditions in which I personally *thrive*. My response to risky or uncertain situations is to improvise. I just make it up as I go, and it generally sounds plausible to others. I have managed to convince hundreds of people to go along for the ride—witness how I managed to convince over 120 people to come on board to make my first movie for FREE. Now, at the time I didn't even realise this was such a useful skill because it came so naturally to me. If I had known I had this skill at the time, I would have bottled it and sold it! However, now that I *do* know, I can consciously use this innate, instinctual talent to create more abundance in my life.

Finally, the Implementor aspect indicates how I handle *space and tangibles*. Guess what? I don't, really. At least not on a practical level—that is, I am not good at dealing with space and tangibles.

However, I *am* good at imagining what the end result would look like. This all figures in to my "make it up as you go" philosophy—and that is something I am very good at. Unfortunately, when I worked in a bank and clients required answers, "make it up as you go" was *not* a good strategy. No wonder I didn't last long there!

So, here's an overview of my Kolbe A Index results: I am *best* with future-oriented challenges and dealing with the essential facts. I don't get bogged down with detailed information. I say, "yes" before even knowing the end of the question, then I turn it into a productive venture. The best way I gather and share information is to simplify it. I adapt situations and events to suit myself. I improvise my way out of things *and* into things. I implement practical things is by imagining what the end result might look like. Pretty much, I have very limited practical skills.

Now, do I feel badly about this? No! We all have different areas of strength—and the real key to living the life you deserve is to *operate from within your areas of strength*. When you are *not* doing so, you will not have *true* wealth, and you will experience your work as difficult or stressful, rather than pleasurable and easy. For example, I spent a large part of my professional life training and working as an accountant. Those job requirements include very practical skills, following rules and regulations. As you can see from my Kolbe A Index—that is exactly what does *not* come naturally to me. The job of an accountant leaves no room for improvising, adapting or imagining better outcomes—those skills which come *most* naturally to me. The result? I felt that I did not fit in. My life was stressful. I did not feel joy in my work; it was difficult rather than easy and joyful. No wonder!

You see, when you are in a profession, job or career in which *learned* skills are the norm, it is very difficult for your *natural* skills to shine through. In fact, having the natural skills that I have was a positive detriment to my existence as an accountant. Now, someone with a Kolbe A Index result pretty much the opposite of mine might well thrive in the accounting profession! For a different person, that profession might feel easy and joyful. The point is this: learned skills can often *mask* natural strengths. Was I able to learn the skills required for a profession in accounting? Sure, I was. But that work did not feel easy and joyful for me because I was not using—or even really aware of— my natural strengths. Instead, I had to utilise *learned* skills every day. When this is the state of your life, you are often made to feel like a failure if you can't conform or if you can't follow the rules of a specific job. On the other hand, when you are using your natural, instinctive abilities and talents, you feel *validated*. Your work feels joyful rather than stressful. Now, obviously the objective is to figure out how, in this life, you can leverage your innate skills to your best advantage.

So, using my Kolbe A Index as an example, we can look at how I might leverage *my* innate skills to my best advantage. Now, I'll be honest. When I first saw the diagram it looked bleak to me. As you can see, it shows that my Mode of Operation is 2(Fact Finder)-3(Follow Thru)-10(Quick Start)-3(Implementor). Clearly, I was a Quick Start and would take action immediately, leaving others in my wake. I had little talent at finding facts or researching, had no follow-through, and had little ability implementing projects. It was looking grim. Every seminar I was going to at that time was about trying to get an Internet business—or *any* kind of business—off the ground. I was hampered by a lack of natural skills to put everything together and to follow through on any of my ideas. In essence, the Kolbe A Index showed me *why* I kept failing at these tasks over the years.

For one thing, these seminars I was going to in order to get a business off the ground were all based on some kind of *system*.

At these seminars, the presenters kept insisting that *if you follow this system you can't go wrong*. For me, wrong strategy! As you see from my Index results, I am not *able* to follow a system. I need help from other people. I need to *create my own system* or to promote others systems, not actually "do" them. I need to be my *own* product, my own brand! No wonder the seminars weren't working for me.

The good news is that the Kolbe A Index celebrates *every skill* and the individual way that each of us operates. So, you see, there *is* a place for everyone and everyone can be in the right place! We just need to realise this, by understanding our natural talents. So, how can I put my talents to best use? Let's look again at each of the four pillars, and examine how I can avoid stress in each mode of operation.

According to the Fact Finder result, I simplify information when I gather it. This means that I generalise, abbreviate, summarise, clarify options and get right to the point. So in order to avoid stress in the Fact Finder MO, I need to avoid writing out details, seeking complex justifications, getting into lengthy debates and re-reading all the fine print. So, I really need a personal assistant who can do all of these things for me. You can imagine how tedious it was for me being an accountant for all those years. How my star did get tarnished!

My mode of Follow Thru is my way of organising things. This means that I need to frequently revise systems, multitask, and deal with tasks as they arise. It is important that I don't try to follow standard methods, and I need to see and be easily able to reach what I use. For example, in my kitchen I have cleaning products sitting on the bench so I can easily use them. On a bench next to the kettle I have teas, coffee, and sugar all laid out so that I can easily choose something. I hate having to *find* things. Essentially, I can avoid stress in the Follow Thru MO by *avoiding* rigid rituals, step- by-step procedures, repeating myself and being overly scheduled. Once again, you can imagine the problems I had with the rigid timetables of the accounting profession— lodgment of documents and taxation forms by certain dates. It was a nightmare. So, in order to follow my Star Profile I need people around me who can do these things. It really takes me out of my flow and takes me into stress mode.

My Quick Start MO, or my way of dealing with risk and uncertainty, is by racing the clock and doing things at the last minute, by innovating changes, by experimenting and by promoting alternatives. I am always looking for different ways, easier ways to do things and I find it hard to follow rules. I can avoid stress in Quick Start MO by *not* conforming, by taking potential risks head on, by not sticking to the script, by not editing my many ideas and by not knowing outcomes. I love a challenge!

My mode of Implementation is my knack for seeing solutions in my mind, visualising possibilities, conceptualising what might be, and making decisions without tangible evidence. This can be a problem when you are trying to explain your actions to someone who is not a Quick Start, e.g. a Bank Manager. So, I avoid stress in the Implementor MO by *not* building physical models, maintaining mechanical equipment, demonstrating the use of tools, or taking things apart or fixing broken parts. During my time as an accountant, I often had to show people how to use various computer programs. My goodness, it was such a strain and an effort! Essentially, I should avoid being responsible for practical, concrete matters. My skill is in imagining, conceptualising, and visualising possibilities— not actually *doing*.

We each have a combination of conative talents that we were born with. We each have equal time and conative energy. Personally, I need to make few commitments and target top priorities. I'm most productive when I am operating with high potential challenges. I work best when considering under-developed and unconfirmed opportunities. I have a vision for the possibilities. I'm one of those people who, when everybody is looking at ABC, I'm asking "what about D?"

How I can personally build on these conative strengths? I need to give myself a deadline and skim the details. I work best by glancing through what needs to be done rather than finding more information to complete a task. If I have a structured format or system to follow, I'm very likely to procrastinate. I need to modify things so that I can accomplish them in my own way. I need to find the freedom within the task to be myself.

My best methods of communication are spoken words, ad libs, improvised metaphors, visuals, bullet points and intense colours… I need to skip the details and get to the bottom line. I like to give an overview. I have found that I can build trust easily with people if I am coming from my essence. People instinctively know when that is happening, and they really do trust me. When I am communicating from my true conative character, others are attracted to me. So, in order for me to succeed, I need to use my conative strengths. My Kolbe MO (mode of operation from my instinctive ability) determines how I will do something.

In order to succeed in a particular environment, we each need a place where our *natural abilities* are nurtured. This means that for true success to emerge, you need to find a place where you are free to be yourself. Personally, I need a place, a career or job that provides me with the opportunities to:

- Deal with change with the freedom to experiment and take significant risks
- Challenge myself with deadlines and tough-to-reach goals
- Thrive on interruptions that create diversity and brainstorming opportunities

I love to create and I love to inspire. I prefer working with large groups rather than one-on-one situations. Starting with the revelation of my Star Profile, I now have a Life Path in which I can use my *natural skills and talents.* Every day now, I get to live my correct earthly career path—my true Life Path as an inspirational teacher.

So, to put all of this in terms of the **5 steps to living the life you deserve**: Using the Wealth Dynamics Profiling System and the Kolbe A Index, I have been **discovering a framework** for my life — one that produces success and abundance, easily and effortlessly. In Step 1, I built my spiritual foundation — because a house cannot stand strong without a foundation. Step 2 has consisted of two parts. First, with the aid of the Wealth Dynamics system, I discovered my true Life Path. My Star Profile means that I rely on my force of personality as the best way to create my wealth—and working as an inspirational teacher fits perfectly.

Then, using the Kolbe A Index, I gained a much better understanding of my natural talents and how I can *use them in service to my Life Path.* I have fine-tuned my strengths within my Star Profile and now I know what I *should* and *should not* be doing to create my wealth. I know what I am good at, and which things cause me undue stress and struggle. There are people out there for whom these tasks come easily and effortlessly—and I should let them do what they are meant to do while I get on with my job.

What does all of this add up to? I understand my true identity, and I hope that I have demonstrated to you how to find yours. By clearly understanding yourself, you can make better choices, *right now*, and shortcut your way to understanding *your* Life Path and life purposes. I promise you, this process is completely liberating! It frees you up to devote yourself to developing your strengths, rather than trying to strengthen your weaknesses.

When you work on your *strengths* rather than your weaknesses, life becomes easier and more joyful! Automatically, you will begin to attract what you need. You will be working from a place of passion, and others will want to be around you—and to pick up the tasks that don't come easily to you.

Learn from my example! (You can find access to these resources on my website.) I implore you to find out where you best fit and what your natural talents are. Once you have done so, you *will* find your flow and create both inner and outer wealth. So go on— get started! Identify your Life Path, discover *your* unique natural talents—start *living the life that you deserve, now!*

6

How to Guarantee Success in Every Area

"What you get by achieving your goals is not as important as what you become by achieving your Goals."
— **Zig Ziglar**

Step 3: Build Your Boundary by Setting Goals

The practice of defining goals dominates the vast body of self-help literature. So much of the work in this genre is consumed with the question of how to make your goals measurable and achievable. It would appear that those who have achieved great success in life have done so by setting goals. Often, those same successful people speak about periods when they did not set goals well, and they counted themselves as failures. Clearly, the evidence appears to weigh in favour of setting goals. That's what this chapter is about. Once you've established the spiritual foundation for your house and constructed a framework by identifying your Life Path, defining your purpose, clarifying who you are and identifying your natural base talents within that path, it's time to go about building your boundary, your fence—and that means setting goals.

The literature tells us that your chances of success are better if you put your goals in writing, and make them specific and manageable. If the goals are large, you should break them down into bite- size pieces. You see, it doesn't help you to set goals that appear out of your reach. If you can't quite see your way clearly to achieving them, you're just setting yourself up for failure and disappointment with yourself. Now, this doesn't mean you can't have a "big picture" in mind. If you're like me, you probably do! But by breaking your goals into smaller bites, you give yourself the chance to feel little successes along the way. As I mentioned in Chapter 2, *success breeds success*— so you need to give yourself the chance to feel it!

Let's take an example of someone who hasn't set any goals previously, but they want to dramatically increase their yearly income. Say they are earning an average yearly income of $40,000. Then they discover the idea of goal setting and want to kick it into overdrive—for example, by saying, "By the end of this year, I will be earning $1,000,000." Now, in essence it is very possible to do that. However, in order to be able to do that you must have *enormous* discipline and focus already as one of your natural gifts. You must be doing daily tasks and techniques in order to radically change many aspects of your life and your environment.

You see, achieving goals is more about mind-set than anything else. In order to achieve big goals, you must change your life. Now, the kind of change I mean is not about faking people out or doing things that feel unnatural to you. In fact, it's just the opposite. It's about reconnecting with your true identity, your own life essence—and in that way *you can change whatever is not working in your life now.*

How do you do this? You start by setting small goals. Little by little, you start to change who you are—by becoming who you *really* are. Every time you achieve one of your small goals, you will feel what success is like. You will stop being so hard on yourself and being caught in negative thought patterns of self-doubt, guilt or shame. You can then move to bigger goals, recognising the feeling of success and getting in touch again with your natural state of joy and self-love. Then, you can go for the big goals. Personally, I'm a big believer in the daily to-do list. Each time you finish one item on that manageable little list, you get to check it off and feel a sense of success.

Remember: no *goal is too small*. It's all about where you are now. One of the reasons I like to make daily lists is that it helps to keep me disciplined, which is one of my hardest life lessons. Maybe it is for you too. Maybe, like me, your mind jumps around all day from one bright shiny object to another, and you have trouble staying focused. Well, if you keep your goals manageable, you will be steadily building up a habit of success. In this way, you will naturally become more disciplined.

The other challenging thing I know personally is that your hard drive may be wired for failure. What I mean by this is: if you haven't had the experience of achieving goals at all, then your body has not been programmed for success. This is hard-core, deep-rooted, DNA level failure I'm talking about. This happens when you have totally lost the plot about what and how to achieve success. Every action that you take leads back to one of failure. Many successful people have attested to long periods of failure of just this kind—until something in them says: "No more!" Now, if you feel that right now your hard drive is wired for failure, I want you to know — *you can always* change that programming.

If you have had some modicum of success in your life, you will be able to do that again. If you haven't, it may be a slightly harder road. But the techniques in the last few chapters of this book *can and will* help you to change your programming. Remember, your *natural state is one of joy*. Success and love *want* to find you. But you will need to clear yourself daily of any negativity. This will help you reconnect with your true inner essence, a sure-fire way to success on any level! Another sure-fire way is to enlist help via a counselor or a coach. This is a more expensive way to do it. However, whichever way you choose, you will definitely need to have some discipline in your life.

Several years ago I attended one of those multi level marketing seminars and the high-powered speaker was up there on stage, energised as all hell, sprouting success, motivation, inspiration and achievement. On one occasion the speaker told a story about how everyone arrives here as a success. You are all already a success because one successful sperm, out of sixty thousand or so, swam its way to one egg and *voila*! Here you are! It sounded ridiculous at the time. However, he was trying to convince everyone, that they had a basis of success already built in from conception and he was trying to get everyone motivated to achieve their goals of financial freedom, having luxury holidays, flashy cars, grand houses and money to burn. Motivation is not the answer. Inspiration is! That's why multi level marketing was not the vehicle for me. You see, those were not my goals. I was not motivated by the speech. I needed something more. I would always start out at those seminars feeling hopeful and enthusiastic—but would end up feeling I didn't quite relate.

What I understand now is that it was too systematised for me; it didn't match my profile type. I needed to create *my own vehicle*; only then could I become totally involved in achieving my dream.

Kathy Kolbe, acclaimed theorist and entrepreneur, has a definition of success that appeals to me. She says: "My definition of success is the freedom to be yourself." How huge is that? If you were free to be yourself, imagine what you could achieve? You would be doing what you love. You would love what you do. Well, that is exactly my goal for you in this book. If you are happy and loving what you do, the money and attachments you need will *come to you*. You will attract all the right people and resources to help you along in your journey. Wow! Wouldn't that be a great goal to achieve? You *can* actually do this if you follow the 5 steps—and gain some traction in your life again. It's not just about succeeding—it's about having fun along the way, too. It's about rediscovering your natural state of happiness. It's actually about love! Love of yourself and others.

Now, goal setting is sometimes pooh-poohed, especially by people who are so-called spiritually inclined. They often say things like: "If it's meant to happen, it will." Or "the universe will provide." There is some level of truth to these claims—but it is not enough to simply believe them. I know, because after I had the successful experience of making my film, I moved toward this type of spiritualism. Basically, by doing this, I "forgot" to set goals. This did not lead to more success for me.

Let me just say, I don't know very many so-called spiritual people who are wealthy. In my opinion, many of them are missing the point and have not connected with all aspects of their lives. You can be wealthy *and* be spiritual. I think sometimes people confuse spirituality with not being materialistic. You can be both. You can be neither. *And* you can be wealthy in *any* aspect of your life. When I use the term "wealthy," I am talking about material and inner—spiritual—wealth both. Some people would like both. True *spiritual wealth* is deep connection with your inner essence, your Higher Self. It also comes from real connection with others.

True outer wealth *stems from* true spiritual wealth. It happens when you have a connection with the Life Path that is right for you. It happens when you have clear life purposes and you're clear about your identity. In this way, you can live a rich and meaningful life on both the inner and outer levels. You can contribute to the world and help others achieve success as well. That's why this is Step 3 of the 5 steps to living the life you deserve: building your boundary by setting goals. In my view, there is no point in setting goals that are not related to moving towards your life purposes. Random goal setting unrelated to your path, your purpose and your inner self are unlikely to be successful. Now, if some of your purposes along the way are to earn more money so that you can stay on your path, then that, to me, is a legitimate goal. It is interconnected to your true life path.

As I mentioned earlier, there was a period in my life when I subscribed to the New Age notions of spirituality. I read about intentions and affirmations—for a while, these were all the rage. Another thing this literature suggested was that by setting goals, you would be limiting yourself and your choices—not keeping options open. Perhaps you've heard the story about the chap who wished for an old horse to help him with his farm work. He prayed for it constantly. So, those in heaven looked down and said: "Well, he asked for that old horse and that's what he'll get. However, we were going to give him two really young horses instead." Too bad for him, right? This is meant to suggest that you limit your choices by having goals that are too specific. My point is this, though: You need to have a bit of discipline to change your life and to recognise success when you come across it on your journey. However, when you add goal setting it *can* change your life dramatically.

Now, looking back over that successful period in my life when I achieved one goal after another in making my movie, I can easily see the key elements that went into my success. One of these? *I had a very clear goal and I wrote it down.* Now, I did not have a specific time or date of achievement, I only knew that it would be in that particular year. I know that this goes against the grain of the hard-core goal-setting fraternity. However, I had secret tools in place that guaranteed my success. The first one was my strong connection with my Higher Self. The second was that I was in the right Life Path; admittedly, by accident—sometimes it works that way. What do I mean by the right Life Path? Life Path is a general direction for your life work based on your natural talents base. It is ingrained. Something that you are born with! Your natural talents do not change. I also had *strong purposes that matched my individual attributes*. Also, I was practicing daily techniques to stay in touch with my natural state of joy, and I behaved with love towards others and myself all the time. We'll discuss these last two aspects in later chapters. For now, suffice it to say that I advocate *writing down your particular goal, in a clear and definite way that explains what you want to achieve.* This is an important element of staying on your Life Path.

When I was making my movie, I only set one goal: to complete the film by the end of that year, easily and effortlessly. I did not see the need at that time to write daily, weekly, or monthly goals. I'll tell you why. My Path was *so clear*—I was coming from a place of *knowing* that I would achieve the end result. This "knowingness" stemmed from my unbreakable bond with my Higher Self.

The Path was this: do the short film course, write the script, get the team, get the actors, find the locations, set a shoot date, find the editing suite, find the sound and put it together. I did keep a to-do list to simplify my days, but I did not actually have to write down my goals after the initial goal. The reason I was so clear? I was hooked into my Higher Self the whole time. In essence, this was my theta place. I asked for things and they just came to me—instantly and without a lot of effort. I was in flow. Being in theta is the state of mind where you are in touch with your Higher Self. Your Higher Self, in turn, will summon all of the available resources from all of the available avenues in this universe and beyond, to help you achieve your goal. My daily to-do lists acted as my mini goals along the way.

In a later chapter we will talk about the theta mind and how to use it effectively, easily and effortlessly to achieve your goals. I also want to make the point that during the making of my film, I was so focused on this one goal that nothing else got in the way. I didn't have any financial, relationship, social, health or other goals competing for my attention at the time. Every ounce of my being was directed towards that one goal of making my movie. I ate it, I dreamt it, and I slept with it. It really was *not possible to fail.* Consequently, when the film ended I was in a state of overwhelm as I had nothing else lined up to take the place of that goal. Yes, it was big fun at the time to achieve that goal! However, a word of caution: if you don't balance other goals in your life so that you always have a direction of focus, the letdown after achieving one big goal can be enormous!

In his book, *Double Your Income by Doing What You Love*, Raymond Aaron describes the following very useful goal-setting practice: Raymond suggests that you write out your goals as though you have *already achieved them.* You do this on a yearly basis. This means that at the end of the year, you write down what you want to achieve as of December 31 of the following year. So it's as though you are looking back at how successful you have already been. Raymond has kindly donated his book as a free bonus for my readers. It is available from my website.

This is exactly what I did when making my movie: I wrote the goal at the end of the previous year as though I had *already* achieved it. I focused on how easily and effortlessly everything came to me. I focused on how it would look and who would come on board. I focused on the feelings of success. My strategies for getting people on board for free—that is, getting a cast and crew who were just doing it for the love of it not for money—manifested immediately. However, I cannot overstate the amount of energy devoted to this one goal. It was life consuming. It can be like that if you love what you are doing and doing what you love. I didn't know that I loved making movies. What I loved doing was creating something out of nothing. That was the success to me. I am highly creative, intuitive and have a powerful ability to inspire people. These are my natural base talents, and maintaining my connection with my Higher Self made sure I kept using them. These were the very elements that led me to achieving my goal easily and effortlessly. I was in flow. The movie making was a coincidence. It could have been another project that utilised my innate skills. It just happened to be about movie making at that time. But now that I know what my innate skills are, I can utilise them to easily achieve other goals in my life. It can be this way for you, too!

Raymond Aaron also offers several other little gems you can implement along the way to keep yourself focused and on track. He has developed specific templates that make it easy to record and collate your goals. He also has some interesting strategies based on MTO. M stands for the minimum, the easy goal that you are likely to achieve easily. T stands for the actual target you are really striving for, one that is hard or bigger that the minimum. O stands for the outrageous, really over-the-top goal that would be amazing if you reached it. This is one that is in the realm of possibility, but outside your actual experience. So, this means you break your goal into three parts: the *minimum* you want to achieve, your *target* goal and the *outrageous* goal that which you don't expect to achieve—but you just might. I have used the MTO strategy for my financial goals for this year.

Now, in order to structure your goals, you might consider doing a range of goals over the spectrum of your life. That is, think about your goals in different categories of life: financial, social, relationship, career/business, spiritual, personal, mental, emotional, health, physical and contribution. It's important at this stage to take into account everything you've figured out so far—your Life Path and life purposes and what your natural talents are. Having more structure in your life gives you greater focus and clarity for your goal, which now needs to be clearly specified. It also means the likelihood of achieving your goals increases exponentially.

Another aspect of prime importance is to discover *what has held you back in the past*. Failure habits can continue to pop up if you don't identify them, and they will surely interrupt your success. You will also need to remember your forgiveness goals, which we'll talk about a bit later. You see, when you succeed, you may not have the skills in place to cope with this newfound success—just as I didn't after the success of making my movie. *Often we are just as afraid of success as we are afraid of failure.* To combat fear of success, you need to ask yourself: Who will I be? Who will I have become when I start seeing success in my life? What will I need to do to maintain my success? We'll look at this crucial element in more detail later on when we do an environmental health check on things that may impede your progress.

A useful strategy for Step 3, building your boundary, is to organise your major goals into three monthly time schedules,

3-monthly, 6-monthly, 9-monthly and yearly. For example, three major goals for each period of four months (about a dozen major goals spread throughout the year). The reason for doing this is so that you can identify little goals on a daily or weekly basis that directly relate to the bigger goal. This way, you can experience small, manageable successes. These could be as simple as learning a new task, taking up a sport, or even clearing out a cupboard. Nothing is too small. Never forget: *success breeds success*. The more small goals you achieve along the way, the more confidence you will have as you head towards the bigger ones.

In Chapters 8, 9 and 10, we will look at some daily techniques to keep you on track, positive, focused, and moving steadily towards your goals. The goals you set will now be relevant to your Life Path and your life purposes. They will be built around your spiritual foundation and will help you to reconnect with your inner self. These techniques are what I used daily to achieve my goal of making a movie. And yes, I use them now. And yes, they work! And no—they do not take up a lot of time!

A word here about time; the rush to achieve things in as short a time as possible is endemic in our society. But what if you have been languishing in a directionless territory, without any goal setting or achievement all of your life? What's your rush? Now, you get to embark on the wonderful journey of setting goals and changing your life bit by bit—in a deep and meaningful way. No real change happens overnight. *Enjoy the journey*. There may be surprising twists and turns along the way that take you in an even better direction than you could have imagined. So yes, set your goals and look forward to achieving them and—above all—have fun!

7

Forgiveness, the Miracle Key

"Enlightenment is an accident, but some activities make you more accident prone."

— **Zen Saying**

Step 4: The Umbrella of Love

Congratulations! At this stage, you have built a wonderful house. Working from your solid spiritual foundation, you have identified the framework of your Life Path and life purposes and clarified your natural talents base. You have found your identity, who you are. Around it all, you have put up the strong fence of your goals. Now, to protect and nurture all that you have built, you need to hold up a big umbrella of love! This principle springs from Step 1—your spiritual foundation. In fact, the umbrella of love is the key tool of *forgiveness*, and it is, really, the umbrella for all of the other steps.

In Chapter 3, I talked about *A Course in Miracles* as my own spiritual foundation. One of the keys to spiritual advancement I discussed was the notion of *separation*—separation from God and therefore from our own spirits. This separation creates a perpetual underlying guilt that we tend to project onto others, creating lives troubled by anger, resentment, self-doubt, and isolation. But it is only the *misperception* of this separation from God that leads us to be separated from our own inner selves, and therefore from one another, as we live in separate bodies, with separate families, separate countries and so on. The underlying truth is that *we are all one*.

Because we have become so separated from each other we often fail to see the beauty within others. Instead, we tend to attack others as though they have sinned against us. We play the blame game and hold grudges, ensnaring them and ourselves in an endless negativity trap. The only way to be *free* of this trap—the only way to free ourselves and those around us—is through the principle of *forgiveness*. If we understand that we are all one and that *God loves us all equally*, and we practice forgiveness at every opportunity, then we will come to see others and ourselves as equals. Only through forgiveness can we come to understand love: of ourselves and of others. So you see, it really is—actually, about love!

In this chapter we will explore exactly what forgiveness is and how it can lead you back to love. Fundamentally, forgiveness allows us to *let go* of negative emotions we may be holding against our *self* or another person. We see the recipient of our anger for who they really are and accept them totally. In essence, forgiveness allows us to see the other person *as* ourselves. It enables us to see that we are all one. Forgiveness is ultimately *a change in perception*. Just as a *miracle* is a change in perception. This is the key: forgiveness invites more miracles into your life. Only through the practice of forgiveness can you open your life up to receive the miracles that await you!

How can you achieve forgiveness? First, you must learn to come from a place of acceptance—of yourself and others. Then, you must practise releasing the negative bond that exists between you and another—or between you and your inner self. Now, as I mentioned earlier, forgiveness does not mean that you must welcome the other person into your life as a friend. Forgiveness, ultimately, *is for you*. It is a move towards true *freedom*. When you release the hold that the ego thought system has over you, then you release your mind at the same time. You free your mind up for more productive tasks. If you continue to hold onto the negative thought or emotion, you are *trapping energy* in two ways. First, your own energy is trapped—which prevents you from living your life to the fullest. Not only that, the other person's energy is caught up in this negative loop as well. Neither of you can be truly free to access your energetic resources and contribute meaningfully to the world. By freeing yourself of anger and resentment, you do a huge *service to all of mankind*. Stopping the pattern of negativity allows both you and the object of your resentment to become engaged in pursuits that are more productive.

I spent much of my life trying to understand my deep-rooted feelings of isolation, of separation from others and myself. It wasn't simply aloofness. I am far from being an aloof person! I just felt on a deep level that *I did not belong here*. I have been through dozens of seminars, presentations, webinars and e-courses in my attempts to find that elusive key—the key that would unlock the door to these feelings of isolation. The motivational speakers I used to see would espouse things like: "let go and let God!" Or: "everything you need you already have!" And so on. These catchy phrases didn't explain my profound sense of separation and I used to look at them in wait for the explanation. I personally don't believe they really understood what they were saying. If they did, they certainly did not know how to explain it.

Finally, through reading *A Course in Miracles* I found the answers! The key to happiness was *right here inside me* all the time, but I didn't know how to get to it. Now I finally understand what forgiveness is and what it can mean for one's spiritual life as well as one's physical life.

As we discussed in Chapter 3, *A Course in Miracles* reveals that Christ, mankind's representative, began thinking of separating from God, his father. These thoughts of separation are the original source of the ego mind. This ego mind of ours is now separated from its *source*—God, our original essence, truth and love. Hence, the ego mind keeps us in a place of non-love, which we call fear or guilt. This underlying guilt about the separation from divinity causes the ego mind to *project* guilt onto others. That is why, when we are operating just from the ego mind, we tend to see *other people as wrong*, as having sinned against us. Often, we also experience feelings of anger with ourselves because of this deep-seated guilt.

When we are coming from this place, we are not seeing the world as it *truly is*. Instead, our minds are filled with all kinds of misperceptions based on the underlying guilt from the separation. These misperceptions are made even worse by our learned behaviours and beliefs from our upbringing and environment. We project our perceptions onto those around us, seeing the negativity that the ego mind *wants* to see. This way of perceiving *only leads to lack*—lack of truth, lack of love. Instead of "perceiving" all the time, then, what if we came from a place of *knowing*? If we came from a place of *knowingness*, we would see the love and truth in others. If we set aside the ego mind, with its painful guilt over the separation, we would only see what is *really there*—the reality that we are all connected and that the universe contains all the abundance we need.

The ego mind was created to cover up our enormous sense of guilt about being different - and therefore separate—from God. The ego mind fears that if you really look inside yourself you will see that there is *nothing to be afraid of*. So, the ego mind keeps you from doing this by maintaining a perpetual negative loop. Under the control of the ego mind, you are cut off from the *right mind*, also called the Holy Spirit. You are cut off from your Higher Self, out of communication. Trapped in the wrong mind, life seems negative, confusing and futile. In reality, the universe is quite the opposite; it is, fundamentally, a place of love and abundance. A shift in your perception is all that is required to experience this.

How does the ego mind keep you from getting back to your Source mind? By telling you that everything that is happening to you comes from all of those bad people outside of you. Rather than looking *inside ourselves*, we project our guilt and the corresponding negative thoughts onto others. The ego mind's job is to recognise sin in others. In this way, we project our guilt externally. The main tool of the ego mind to keep you externally focused is *anger*. When you get angry you attack or you defend. As soon as you do this, someone becomes a victim. The victim's job is to blame external forces, people, and situations for their lot in life. So instead of *releasing* these negative thoughts and feelings, the victim remains trapped in rage and blame, missing the real state of healing and abundance that is just beyond the veil of his illusion. The external projections of the ego mind's fear manifest as: anger, bitterness, resentment, depression and repression, self-punishment, doubt, judgment, any sense of lack, shame, and guilt.

By maintaining anger, you become easily hooked into a web of stories to support that anger. Sometimes others support you in your stories; they agree with you that you have a *right to be angry*. The truth is: *No one* has a right to be angry with one of God's creations. When you are angry with another human, you are angry with God. You are angry with yourself. Think of all the ramifications. As you practise more anger and feel more justified in maintaining the rage, just notice *how and what your life becomes*. You may constantly carry around resentment; you may feel sad or depressed, helpless and hopeless. Carrying these dark feelings all the time, you may well have *stopped* attracting abundance and *started* attracting lack. When we attract lack, it seems like we are always poor, just barely managing to hold it together.

If you find that you are unable to manifest all the good that you desire in your life, it means that you are *holding negativity* in your being. This negativity may be in the form of old resentments, misperceptions about another, old belief systems, emotional traumas or perhaps a combination of all these things. Only when you release this negativity will the cloud of doom lift off you. Through forgiveness, you will begin to attract the love and abundance of the universe!

Unfortunately, the concept of true forgiveness often goes against the grain of what humans have been taught. Based on our own internal perceptions and the general rules of society, we automatically feel attacked if someone does wrong by us. As soon as we feel attacked, we are in defence mode and we start slinging back the negativity. Our opponent responds in kind. Thus we begin a vicious circle of lack of love! *We can never win by doing this.*

Ultimately, forgiveness means that we are not justified in being angry with others or ourselves *for any reason whatsoever*. We must learn to love and let live. To let go and let God! That's right. We need to let our inner selves shine through and turn the other cheek. We must learn to see the goodness that is essentially in all of us—the fundamental divine essence that connects us to God *and* to one another.

I call forgiveness the umbrella of love because it is a *new way of living*—one that encompasses everything. With forgiveness, I live every day under the protection of the umbrella of love.

This means that my first thoughts about others and myself are thoughts of love. No longer will I perpetuate my thoughts of sin and guilt against others. I will release these things in order to live life in a new way— in touch with the *reality* of love and abundance that is the true state of the universe.

So how can we *put into practice* this thing called forgiveness? According to *A Course in Miracles*, the practice of forgiveness requires that we accept "the atonement." This is another way of saying that yes, we have made an error *of judgment* about our self or another and we are willing to see things differently. To do this, you ask your Higher Self to help you *change your perception* about the person or situation. In this way, you open the door to let in truth—the truth that we all have, at our core, a place of love. Even though it may not always feel like it—we are all one. You *free* yourself by realising this.

To practise forgiveness, you must ask your Higher Self, "Please help me change my perception about this person and what I perceive they did to me." As soon as you find yourself thinking things such as: "he shouldn't have…" you know you have a perception error to address. When you feel that someone is attacking you—or vice versa—remind yourself, "But God loves them too!" If you keep repeating this, you will bring yourself back to an understanding about the *connection* you share with the other person. Thus, you will break the habit of misperception. You need to remind yourself that perhaps the person is making an error, and not a sin against you. In this way, they have a chance to correct their error without all of the guilt and attack that goes on in a continuing battle of "I am right and you are wrong."

Our lives are combinations of a series of perceptions. In many ways, we live our lives in our *heads*, filtering everything through our belief system, our environment, our emotions, and our memories. We project our thoughts onto the world in such a convincing way that we actually see the world *as we have perceived it*. We tend to think *everyone* sees the world the same way we do. This is not the case! With so many individual perceptions going on all the time, how difficult real communication is! Our chances to really be on the same page with one another are limited; the margin of error in *interpretation* is huge.

The chance that we will interpret the external party, as being wrong or bad, as doing something against us, is very high. However, what we do from there is up to us. We tend to try to justify our perceptions by placing blame on to others, through the tool of anger. Anger keeps us bound to the wrong mind, the ego mind. The ego mind's job is to maintain the separation that is to eventually destroy us. And it is working extremely well. So, in order for us to be able to correct our errors we need to have a willingness to forgive.

Dr Hawkins has written an amazing book called *Power versus Force*, whereby he uses kinesiology to establish truth on the planet. He has developed a scale to indicate the state of our human evolution at this point in time. Dr Hawkins' findings indicate that at present 85% of the planet are living in fear, doubt, anger, judgment and criticism—every possible scenario of lack there is. This means that *the ego mind is winning*. Apparently, the ego mind is doing its job of keeping us separate from our rightful position—our true essence of love. At this rate, the possibility of us all overcoming our errors of perception and finding our way back to love seems a long way off.

So, you might ask, "How can I free myself of this negativity and move towards my essence, the truth within me, which is my natural state?" Firstly, you have to make a *conscious decision* that you want to change. You then need to *be more aware* of what is happening in your life and your relationships. If you observe a pattern in your life, you must examine it. For example, my experience has been, every time I am in a new place of work, someone "does something to me", and I feel threatened and ostracised. This might go on for some period of time and then I leave. But the scenario *keeps happening* to me.

If something keeps happening "to you," it means you have no control over your thoughts and actions. You are merely being buffeted about at the whim of your ego mind. If you want to live more consciously, you must examine these kinds of situations and change *how you perceive* what is happening to you. In this way, you can take charge of your life again and make things happen to you by choice and by design. You need not live at the mercy of others or of your own misperceptions.

You need to take charge. Examine the situation and ask yourself what is happening. Ask to see what your part in the drama was. Then, ask your Higher Self to help you change your perception about this situation. Next, you can use a technique to intervene with the principle of forgiveness until the emotional charge on the issue has been dispelled. In the upcoming chapters, I will talk about some of these physical techniques you can use to bring forgiveness into your life.

You may well say, "But, he did this to me and I have a *right* to be angry." *A Course in Miracles* asks the essential question, "Do you want to be *right* or *happy*?" You can maintain your anger and be right, certainly. Or, you can forgive and be happy. It's always your choice.

I can assure you that once you experience how powerful it is to just *let go* of any hatred or other negativity you are holding, you will want to *speed up the process*. You will want to have this liberating experience every day! That is why later in the book I will share with you some daily techniques you can use just for this purpose.

Remember, forgiveness is not about the other person. It is about *you*. It is *for* you. Forgiveness allows you to *release the hold* that your negative thought has over you. It's about choosing a more powerful position. At the same time, forgiveness releases the other person as well and allows *both* of you to heal. This is what the universe wants—healing and love. It is our true human birthright—and forgiveness is the way back.

Forgiveness is a process and can take time, depending on the circumstance. According to *A Course in Miracles*, all you need is a little *willingness*. This does not mean a huge desire to feel totally forgiving and loving. It just means the bare minimum of wanting to do this. The process of forgiveness is simple but actually doing it is not necessarily easy. You may find large pockets of resistance on some issues and with some people. In some cases, you may not be ready to forgive. Eventually, though, you will see how much joy and spiritual lightness the practice of forgiveness brings. In time, it will become easier and easier.

I must say the practice of forgiveness was difficult for me at first. It literally took me days to forgive the first time—days of repeating the word "forgiveness" over and over again. This process can work, but I have discovered another technique that seems to work a lot faster. In Chapter 9, we will look at a technique that speeds up your forgiveness recovery. You will know when you have achieved forgiveness because you will feel *different*. Lighter. Happier. Abundance will take the place of lack. With this umbrella of forgiveness over everything, you will find your way back to *feeling the love* — for yourself and others.

Colour My World (Daily Techniques)

"When you determine what you want. You have made the most important decision in your life. You have to know what you want in order to attain it. "

— **Douglas Surton**

Step 5: Keeping Your House in Order
Part I: The Chakras

These next three chapters all focus on **Step 5 of the five steps to living the life you deserve, now**!—*keeping your house in order.* Now that you have laid a spiritual foundation, discovered your framework and built your fence, it's important to keep this lovely house of yours in order. This means establishing a daily practice to keep you connected to your Higher Self, your spirit. Staying in touch with your Higher Self helps you to stay on the right Life Path and ensures that you are maximising your natural talents to create true wealth, both inner and outer. In this chapter, I will go over some daily techniques you can use to *stay connected to spirit and to clear away any limiting information or beliefs.*

An important part of keeping your house in order is to sweep away useless debris. Accordingly, you can use daily cleansing rituals to clear away any general negativity from your aura or your chakras. Maintaining a practice of the following techniques allows you to gradually improve the strength of your intuition, which in turn keeps you alert to receive messages from your Higher Self. This type of intuitive, ongoing communication with spirit shortcuts the time it takes to reach those goals you set for yourself in Chapter 6. You see, your *spirit* can tell you how to stay on the right Path—as long as you are open and ready to listen.

I originally learnt these techniques in the Higher Consciousness Course and have since come across them in other helpful literature. Colour Therapy—the use of visualising colour as a way of clearing your chakras—is the basis of all of the techniques in this chapter. Colour visualisation is a powerful tool that heightens our senses, our imagination, and our intuition. Colour Therapy performs the very important function of *clearing negativity from your aura*. Clearing away negativity, releasing anger and fear, keeping that umbrella of forgiveness above all that you do—this is how you stay in touch with your Higher Self. This is how you get *back to love*.

So, Colour Therapy assigns each chakra a related colour. These colours and descriptions may vary across cultures, and there is even slight variation in the number of chakras described in different traditions. However, the important thing is that *chakras do exist and they have a powerful spiritual meaning*. Even scientific research has confirmed the existence of chakras. We *can* cleanse our chakras, individually or all at once, and in doing so we keep ourselves aligned, free of negativity, joyful — *in flow*.

For the purposes of these exercises, we will define seven chakras and the corresponding colours that may be associated with each one.

The Chakras

First Chakra: This is the base chakra, and it is located at the root of your torso. This chakra is a centre for support and grounding, which we associate with primal elements such as sexuality and survival. The colour associated with this chakra is red. Also included in these red shades are browns and pinks. This chakra represents our foundation, our instincts, our grounding and our sense of security.

Second Chakra: This is our emotional centre. It is located in the lower abdomen, beneath the navel, and is associated with various shades of orange. When this chakra is open, it gives us a clear connection to our feelings, our desires and to movement.

Third Chakra: This chakra connects us to our decision-making abilities as well as our instincts. It is located in the solar plexus, above the navel. When you make a decision "from your gut," it is coming from this chakra. It is represented by various shades of yellow and is connected with our identity. When it is open and clear, we are operating from a place of great power and energy.

Fourth Chakra: This is the heart chakra, representing feelings of love and security. It is associated with various shades of green. Connection with our heart chakra allows us to love deeply, feel compassion and have a sense of self.

Fifth Chakra: Located in the throat, this chakra represents communication. It is represented by shades of blue. When this is open, we are connected to our creativity and powers or communication. This chakra is also particularly sensitive to sound vibration.

Sixth Chakra: This is known as the third-eye chakra and it is located on the forehead, between and slightly above the eyes. This chakra, represented by shades of indigo, connects us with our intuition. It opens up our psychic abilities, connecting us to levels of information beyond the tangible.

Seventh Chakra: The crown chakra, located just at or above the crown of the head, represents our mental abilities, including knowledge, focus and direction. This Chakra includes shades of purple. It is our connection to our universal identity. When developed, open and clear, this chakra is our source of knowledge, understanding and spiritual connection.

Throughout this chapter, we will be using various colours to describe or attune to the chakras. If you feel the urge to use colours other than the ones I suggest at any point, feel free. The shift in colours you may wish to visualise will depend on how you feel, on what you're trying to achieve. For example, if you feel you are in need of more grounding and you are focusing on your stomach chakra, you may wish to infuse a deeper shade of brown into the yellow. In this way, you consciously visualise a deepening of the colour or hue in order to give you a better sense of grounding.

The purpose of these daily exercises is to fine-tune your senses and open up the channels of communication between yourself and your Higher Self. Thus, you are always in control of your visualisation experience and you may adapt it as you feel is necessary in order to allow messages from your Higher Self to reach you. In this way, you will make a deep connection to your inner self, opening yourself to experience more peace and joy in your life. These exercises provide clear and pleasant ways to *keep your house in order*; in other words, to keep you on track and maintain the five steps to living the life you deserve!

In this chapter, we will look at the following techniques:

Number 1: White Light Cleansing, which is the basis of all of the other techniques.
Number 2: Daily Intention
Number 3: Cleansing Individual Chakras
Number 4: The Sea of Abundance
Number 5: Guided Meditation

It is both easy and pleasurable to incorporate these practical tools into your day. Over time, they will become a part of your daily routine that you look forward to, because they are designed to be relaxing, cleansing and joyful. Too often, people put off being happy until sometime in the future. For example, you might say to yourself, "I'll be happy when I retire; I'll be happy as soon as I earn more money. I'll be happy when the kids get through school," or the like. Using these daily tools can provide a wonderful moment of simple happiness *now. Today.*

These techniques are designed to help you stay on the right Life Path and maximise joy and abundance in your life—materially, emotionally and spiritually. I have observed that *people are afraid of success or failure equally.* For this reason, it can be difficult to stay on the right Path even after you have discovered it. Fear of success shows up in the form of self-doubting questions like, "Will I have to hurt others in order to succeed? Will I lose my friends? Will I be able to sustain success? Do I have the qualities necessary to deserve this success?" Perhaps these questions sound familiar to you. The common thread among all of them is this idea that somehow we are not worthy, that we do not deserve to succeed. Now, if you understand that *we are all one* and that you are, therefore, worthy and deserving of joy, you will not be plagued with these questions. These daily techniques and practices give you the tools you need to keep yourself clear of negative thinking and self- doubting. They help keep you connected with your inner self—the core of *goodness* that we each possess, which is the true source of success.

Life is not a dress rehearsal. We should treat this life as the only life we have. Whether your ambitions for this life are very grand or very humble, you can experience the feeling of success. And once you do, it will come more easily the next time around. Remember, the universe fundamentally *wants* good things to happen to you. You can keep yourself open to those opportunities every day by maintaining a clear connection with your spirit. Day by day, the work—and the abundance—come more and more easily. So *enjoy*!

1. White Light Cleansing

Use this technique daily, when you wake up just to set your day on track, and do before any of the other techniques that we will use later on.

Step 1: Cutting the ties that bind - Sitting upright with your feet on the ground (you could sit in bed), close your eyes and take an imaginary pair of large scissors and cut all around you. What you are doing is cutting the ties that bind you to the past and present. You are also cutting off attachment to negativity in all areas of your life. Feel the feelings as you do this process.

Step 2: Washing through with white light - With your eyes closed, make a shower of sparkling pure white crystal light enter through the top of your head. Make it swirl round like a twister or a hurricane so it spins round in your head. You spin this white light right down through your body and right down through each leg. You are cleaning the gunk out of your body and your aura. You then catch the gunk coming out the bottom of your feet with a large balloon or bag and tie it off. Make it drift off into the universe. You then burst the balloon or bag so that the gunk dissolves back into the universe. You repeat the whole of this step two more times, washing through with the light and catching the gunk.

The White Light Cleansing technique is very simple but hugely powerful. We will use this process at the start of all other techniques.

2. **Daily Intention**

Step 1: Do White Light Cleansing First

Step 2: Then place a large imaginary bubble around yourself so that you are in the centre of it and set your intentions of the day. Your intention might be that you will feel happy and prosperous all day. Just pick one that seems appropriate and if you are going for an interview you might have the intention that the interview will go extremely well for you.

Step 3: In the bubble, sprinkle gold dust all over yourself and state: "Everything I touch turns to gold." Now breathe in the gold dust into your body so that your cells and your DNA tingle with abundance. Feel the feelings.

Step 4: Next sprinkle a beautiful sky blue colour all over you and breathe it in. As you do so say to yourself: "My communications today, with myself and others, will be easily understood and will be rich and meaningful." Feel the feelings.

Step 5: Enclose the outside of your bubble in a band of beautiful cotton candy pink. As you do so say to yourself: "For everyone I meet today, or come into contact with, I will feel love, harmony, peace and balance." Feel the feelings.

Step 6: To seal off your intention and keep you in that bubble of positivity and love all day take three individual gold hoops, one at a time, and make them spin around the bubble like a hula hoop that is dying. Feel the feelings of love and protection from harm. In this way you will lock in your intention, you will keep yourself from harm's way, keep out any negativity from entering your aura and this will protect you during the day.

The White Light Cleansing technique is something that you can use every day to you set yourself on track. The habit of cleansing yourself every day of negativity is just so huge if you can imagine what it does for you in the end. This is what I recommend you do every day to keep you on track and to set yourself up for future success. It just takes you moments and it enhances your feelings of wellbeing and gratitude and fine-tunes your senses. Adding an intention helps you focus on getting what you want.

3. **Cleansing Individual Chakras**

    Step 1: Do the White Light Cleansing process first. This will enable you to recognise the existence of any residual blockage in any area of your aura or in a specific chakra.

    Step 2: Identify the specific area of the blockage. For example, I am highly sensitive to the Solar Plexus area, the third chakra, and I often need cleansing in that particular area. For me, this is how my Higher Self communicates with me most often. It often manifests in that I am unable to make a quick decision about something, or I feel that there must be a better way.

To give you a personal example, I was recently attending an overseas seminar and the organisers suggested that we book into the hotel where the seminar was to be held. I went to the website to book and found that the room rate was much higher than I had anticipated. I rang and asked them if they had a better rate and a smaller room. The room they had could accommodate five people. I only wanted a single room for myself. I went to the website several times to book. I kept saying to myself: "There has to be somewhere else. There has to be a better rate." Then I did this process, individual chakra cleansing.

I visited the hotel website to book several more times and even entered my credit card details, right up to the point of verification. Then I backed out. I asked my Higher Self to send me some information. I remembered a time when a similar situation had arisen and the organisers of a particular seminar had booked a block of rooms. The rate was not what I wanted to pay. I waited and asked for guidance. I found accommodation just next door to the expensive hotel and the seminar for around one third of the price.

Once I had remembered this previous situation I asked my Higher Self for a similar outcome for my present decision. You guessed it! Four blocks down from the expensive hotel and the seminar I found accommodation for less than one quarter of the price.

This is an example of being in tune with your inner guidance. I simply did the individual chakra cleansing process for the Solar Plexus area. I did not need to meditate or go into theta. I just focused on what I wanted and a similar successful time was brought to mind. I was then able to ask for a repeat of that successful outcome. These little wins give you an amazing feeling of abundance. I was so happy for hours afterwards I kept saying to my Higher Self: " Thank you. Thank you. Thank you. I am so happy."

Step 3: Infuse the blocked chakra with a colour. For the third chakra breathe into your body through the top of your head the colour yellow. Concentrate the colour in the solar plexus area. Feel the colour healing you of your dilemma or your blockage. Feel the feelings. Feel the blockage dissipate.

Another way to do this process and to help sensitise your hands for healing, breathe the colour in through the top of your head to fill your body. Hold one hand within eighteen inches of the blocked chakra. Make the colour go down the arm and into the hand. Imagine the colour radiating from your hand and into the blocked chakra. In this way you can feel the concentration of the colour easily.

Step 4: If the intensity of your blockage does not clear entirely, repeat the first 3 steps.

4. **The Sea of Abundance**

You can do this technique at any time during the day to clear yourself of negativity or stress, adjust a change in mood at any time, or to feel abundant. It is quite easy to do and it is very successful.

Step 1: **Do the white light cleansing as above** (you do not need to add the intention).

Step 2: **Surround yourself in a particular colour**: It's as though you are floating in a sea of colour, the Sea of Abundance. Depending on what you are trying to achieve, this will determine what colour you will choose. For example, if you are stressed out, you might make the colour green so that you have more love for yourself in a particular situation.

If you need to be able to communicate with someone at work more easily, you might choose your colour to be blue.

If you are trying to choose between two different options or make a difficult decision, your sea might be yellow. If you want to see more money or abundance in your life, you could use a gold colour.

It is really up to you what colour you choose.

Step 3: **Having chosen your colour lie back in your sea of abundance**: Float and breathe in the colour so that it saturates your whole body. As you do so feel the positive emotions of what you are trying to achieve. For example, if I'm requiring more abundance in my life, I will feel positive, I would feel gratitude and I will feel prosperity as I breathe in and out.

Feel the feelings of success at having achieved whatever you are after. Saturate your cells and your DNA with this wonderful feeling of positiveness and abundance. Float there as long as you need to, it may take minutes or it may be seconds.

This is a hugely powerful technique to get you back on track if you feel any negativity during the day. Just remember to do the white light cleansing before any of the techniques.

5. Guided Meditation

Guided meditation is where someone leads you through a process which engages the senses and makes the meditation an experience. Engaging the senses brings the journey to life and gets you more involved. It fine-tunes the senses for heightened awareness, so that you are connecting more with your innate centre, your core.

For a guided meditation, you will need to listen to a tape, MP3 or a CD so that the voice is guiding you to feel, see, or do specific actions. A normal meditation is one where you listen to some easy music or being in a quiet place, to slow down the beta brainwaves for a set time. In meditation, in order for it to be more meaningful for you, you need to heighten your senses and become more aware. You can get in touch with your Higher Self using these guided meditation techniques. You will achieve easily and effortlessly, everything that you need, when you reconnect with spirit.

Listening to someone else guide you in your imagery and senses is much easier to do than trying to do it yourself. Because the process is achieved by actually doing it, rather than trying to explain it on paper, I suggest that you obtain a copy of a guided meditation, which are freely available on the internet.

What we are trying to do here with these daily techniques is to help you get in touch with your Higher Self more easily. Being able to recognise your Higher Self speaking, your other self, your spirit, helps you to focus on your spiritual path and spiritual purpose and rapidly speeds up the process of finding your true human life path, your identity and your human life purpose. In the next chapter, we will be looking at a technique for achieving forgiveness in your life, for many situations, person, or event.

Creating Forgiveness (Daily Techniques)

"Tapping is just the quickest, easiest, most reliable way that I've found to activate the bodies releasing mechanism."

— **Anon**

Step 5: Keeping your House in Order; Part II: Tapping

In this chapter, I'll talk about a daily technique you can use called Tapping. This is the short name for a healing process called Emotional Freedom Technique, or EFT. It helps you stay connected to spirit and clear away any limiting information and beliefs.

With EFT, you learn to tap upon different acupressure points—or meridians—on your body. The effect is to dissipate negative feelings or beliefs that may be *trapped* in these different locations of the body. You see, our body's energy system can easily become blocked in certain locations— all ancient Eastern medicine is in fact based upon this principle. Essentially, when your energy becomes blocked, you begin to emanate negative emotions. EFT allows you to *release the blocked or trapped energy* and, along with it, the negativity.

Over the last 25 years, Gary Craig has developed the technique I will describe here. The tapping sequence is so simple that anyone can follow it. Many people—including myself—swear by it! If you feel you need additional help or you'd like to work with a practitioner, I recommend Andrew Lewis. You can find his website in the Resources Page at the end of this book or you can download the helpful bonuses he has donated for you on my website.

Part of the reason EFT is so popular is that you don't need any needles to do it, and you can do it yourself at home. However, it is based on the same principles as acupuncture, and works with the same points on the body. With EFT, you simply tap on these acupuncture points to release blocked energy trapped in your body. You can use this technique for *anything* that you need to let go of.

As you recall from Chapter 3, I experienced a revelation when reading *A Course in Miracles*, and that book became the foundation for my spiritual purpose on this planet. The cornerstone of *ACIM*— and of my 5 steps to living the life you deserve—is the idea of *forgiveness*. For true spiritual peace to occur, it is imperative that we learn to forgive—others as well as ourselves. After reading *A Course In Miracles*, I was still at a loss as to *how* to do this, though. Frankly, there were some pretty deeply buried issues getting in the way of my releasing negativity.

I understood that I needed to find my way to forgiveness, but I couldn't quite see my way to it. I needed a specific tool, which *ACIM* did not provide. Yes, I had tried repeating the word "forgiveness" when issues arose and then working through the issues that kept coming up. But this process took days and days to do! I needed a shortcut.

I believe that guilt is the deeper emotion underlying any difficulty we might experience with forgiveness. In my quest for a technique that could dissolve trapped feelings of guilt, I came across EFT. However, there was nothing in the literature specifically related to releasing guilt, so I created some statements myself specifically designed for the purpose. Using the EFT procedure as a basis, I came up with statements to use while tapping on the various pressure points. The result? I have had *enormous success* with this technique releasing guilt, anger, shame, and self-pity—all those deep-seated negative emotions that get in the way of forgiveness. *This is my shortcut for you.* Using EFT regularly, you will feel these negative emotions simply dissolve, making room for forgiveness to enter right away.

As I have said, I initially used EFT as an avenue for reaching a place of forgiveness. However, I have since discovered that this technique can be used for *any area* of your life: physical, emotional, mental, financial, spiritual, relationship or social. The power of tapping to release blocked energy is unlimited! I have used it to address pain in my body such as a sore back or aching feet. I have found that it can release any negativity that is leading to pain or stress in the body. Truly, it is amazing!

At times, if the issue is not resolved after an initial session, this means there may be an even deeper, underlying issue. You may have to dig deeper by re-working the statement to get at the root cause. You can adjust the statements yourself with guidance of your Higher Self or an EFT therapist, if you feel you need more support. Eventually, you can get the sore muscles or the stress to dissolve completely. You will know when your issue has cleared because the negative feeling will *dissipate*, reduce in intensity, or *disappear*.

This diagram is freely available on the internet and it shows the acupressure points on the body and lists the steps and points that we will use in our tapping procedure to help alleviate your emotional issues.

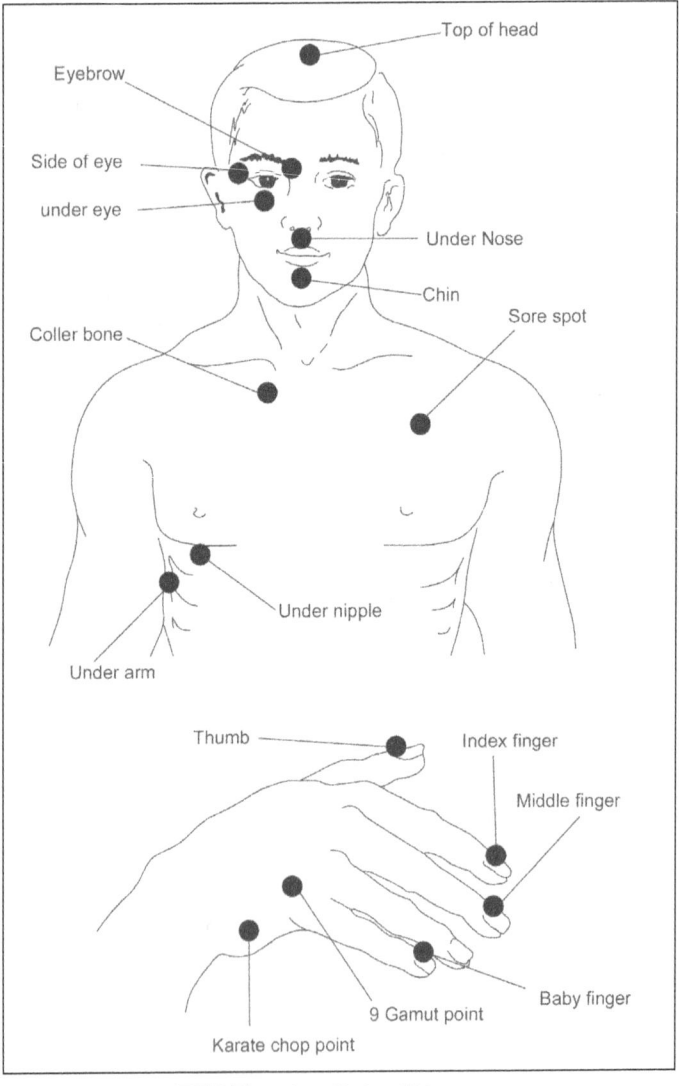

EFT Tapping Point Diagram

An overview of the EFT procedure:

1. **Identify your issue**: this means clearly stating your issue, something that affects you, and can be physically felt in your body.
2. **Evaluate the issue**: this means giving it a mark out of 10 for intensity. So if it is a strong feeling it could be close to 10 and if it's not a strong feeling it could be close to 1.
3. **Say your affirmation**: and the affirmation statement is as follows:
   "Even though I have this............................, I deeply and greatly love and approve of myself
4. **Do the tapping sequence**: the literature is quite diverse on this aspect, as there is no set order for the tapping sequence. Nor is there a set number of taps that you do on each point.
5. **Re-evaluate**: having done the tapping procedure through once, re-evaluate the intensity of the feeling that you have in your body. If it is reduced a little but is still there, you will repeat the above.

This is a general outline of what you do. What I will outline now is the actual tapping sequence that I do as I say my affirmation.

An Overview of the physical Tapping sequence:

Start the process as outlined above to identify your issue and recognise the intensity of it. Outline your affirmation. I use this tapping sequence and find it works well. I personally tap both sides of the body at once at each individual point, when appropriate. I feel that I have more than covered the issue by doing this. At the end re-evaluate the intensity and repeat the process where necessary.

1. **Start at the Karate Chop Point**: Start with one hand, say your issue all the way through, tap with three middle fingers. At the end of the tapping procedure, breathe in and out as though you are letting go of the issue. Repeat the process on the other hand. They call this the set-up. It is where you get your body ready to clear the issues.

Sometimes doing an extensive statement at the Karate Point will clear the issue completely or reduce the issue intensity. Others start at the Sore Spot and either rub this or tap this spot whilst repeating their statement. I tend to use only the Karate Point as my starting place.

2. **Tapping on the crown: with both hands** and with the three middle fingers of each hand, tap on your crown saying your affirmation all the way through. At the end of the tapping procedure, breathe in and out as though you are letting go of the issue.

Using the three middle fingers of each hand, when appropriate, ensures that you cover the meridian or acupressure point.

3. **Go to the eyebrow point on both sides of the face**: Tap, on both sides of the face at once, using the three middle fingers of both hands, say your affirmation all the way through. At the end of the tapping procedure, breathe in and out as though you are letting go of the issue.

4. **Next go to the side of the eye point on both sides of the face**: Tap, on both sides of the face at once, using the three middle fingers of both hands, say your affirmation all the way through. At the end of the tapping procedure, breathe in and out as though you are letting go of the issue.

5. **Then go to the under eye point, on both sides of your face:** Tap, on both sides of the face at once, using the three middle fingers of both hands, say your affirmation all the way through. At the end of the tapping procedure, breathe in and out as though you are letting go of the issue.

6. **Next go to the under nose point, using only one hand:** Tap just under the nose and above the top lip with one hand, say your affirmation all the way through. At the end of the tapping procedure breathe in and out as though you are letting go of the issue.

7. **Then go to the chin point, using only one hand:** Tap the point under the bottom lip and half way between the bottom lip and the base of the chin with one hand, say your affirmation all the way through. At the end of the tapping procedure, breathe in and out as though you are letting go of the issue.

8. **Next go to the collar bone point, on both sides of your body** just under the beginning of the collarbone: Tap, on both sides of the body at once, using the three middle fingers of both hands, say your affirmation all the way through. At the end of the tapping procedure, breathe in and out as though you are letting go of the issue.

9. **Then go to the under nipple point, on both sides of the body**, just beneath the breast in the crease: Tap, on

both sides of the body at once using the three middle fingers of both hands, say your affirmation all the way through. At the end of the tapping procedure, breathe in and out as though you are letting go of the issue.

10. **Next go to the under arm point, on both sides of your body**, down the line of the side of your body, just below the armpit: Tap, using the three middle fingers of both hands , tap on both sides of your body at once, say your affirmation all the way through. At the end of the tapping procedure, breathe in and out as though you are letting go of the issue.

There are two ways to tap at the under arm point. Do one side with one hand and tap, and then do the other side with the other hand. The tapping point is right at the side of your body. For women it is easy to identify because it is at the edge of the bra cup line. The way I do it is a cross my arms over the front of my chest and then I tap both sides with both hands at once using the three middle fingers on both hands, saying my affirmation all the way through. If you use the three fingers all the time when you are tapping you will find that you will cover the acupressure point easily. So do not be concerned that you're not tapping in the right place.

11. **The next point is the side of the top of the thumb, using one hand at a time:** Turn your hand on the side with your thumb facing towards you. At the side of the top of the thumb take two fingers, the index and the middle fingers of the other hand, and tap on the side of your thumb, say your affirmation all the way through. At the end of the tapping procedure, breathe in and out as though you are letting go of the issue.

Repeat the process on the other hand.

12. **The next point is the index finger, using one hand at a time:** With your hand on its side facing towards you, tap your index finger with two fingers on the point, say your affirmation all the way through. At the end of the tapping procedure, breathe in and out as though you are letting go of the issue.

    Repeat the process on the other hand.

13. **The next point is the middle finger, using one hand at a time:** Tap the middle finger point with your two fingers, and say your affirmation all the way through. At the end of the tapping procedure, breathe in and out as though you are letting go of the issue.

    Repeat the process on the other hand.

14. **The next step is the baby finger point, using one hand at a time:** Tap the baby finger point with your two fingers, and say your affirmation all the way through. At the end of the tapping procedure, breathe in and out as though you are letting go of the issue.

    Repeat the process on the other hand.

This is the entire tapping process. Some people shorten the steps and tap only on specific points instead of using the fourteen points. A little later on we will look at what you might do if your issue has not abated.

Next, we will look at using the Tapping Procedure and Sequence specifically for forgiveness issues.

An example of an Issue of Forgiveness:

So let's now use an example specifically for a forgiveness issue. Say you were angry with spouse for not cleaning up the mess that they had made even though you had asked them to and it is bothering you enormously. In order to activate EFT and start the forgiveness process and the healing process and in order for you to be able to release this issue so that you feel good about yourself and others, this is what I would do. Define the issue:

Say Your Initial Statement:

"Even though I am angry at Ted for not cleaning up the mess when I asked and I don't feel that I should have to, he should know that I am angry with him and that it is bothering me enormously,

Then add these sentences:

I am willing to release these things

I am willing to release the underlying emotional issues

I am willing to release the guilt that this represents and forgive myself and others and

I deeply, greatly and completely, love and approve of myself."

This is an exact example of a statement that you might use when you want to forgive yourself or someone else for something. Remember forgiveness is for yourself so that you feel better and you release the negative energy that binds you to the other person. It's not about them. However, it has the added bonus of releasing the other person so that they can also move forward in their lives.

Another example:

Say you have withheld love in a situation and you have been berating yourself, putting yourself down and self-punishing over the issue. This is what you might say:

> *"Even though I am angry at myself for hating Sue and withholding affection and attention and doubting her feelings for me,*
>
> *I am willing to release these things*
>
> *I am willing to release the underlying emotional issues*
>
> *I am willing to release the guilt that this represents and forgive myself and others and*
>
> *I deeply, greatly and completely, love and approve of myself."*

As I said above you can instigate a shortcut process as follows.

A Short Cut Process:

Instead of tapping the whole six line statement at each point, you can say a few words of your statement at each point, making sure you do at least seven taps on each point.

The other shortcut you can take is just to tap one side of your body instead of tapping both sides. I personally prefer to say the whole statement all the way through whilst tapping each point individually. And I prefer to do both sides of the body at the same time.

What if my issue is not totally cleared?

What happens if I have done this tapping once or twice all way through and I still feel angry and the intensity hasn't reduced more than two points out of ten? I recognise that I still have residual negative feelings.

Sometimes, when we are trying to overcome a deep-seated emotion, we may have competing beliefs within ourselves. On the one hand, you want something to happen and on the other hand, you might not want to have this particular outcome. In some literature, this is called the "psychological reversal" or "secondary gain" in other literature. In this case, another procedure that I have used to great benefit on myself, and you will get a much quicker result if you do this also, is to use The Gamut Point procedure. So, having tapped all the way through a couple of times and you still noticed that the intensity is still evident to a high degree, this is what I would use.

Gary Craig stated that this procedure is generally only needed for 30% of cases. This is to be used after you have used the general tapping procedure. I have found it to be of enormous benefit with lots of issues, particularly physical issues, when there is a residue of negativity which is resisting release. You can do this on one hand and then go and repeat on the other hand if need be.

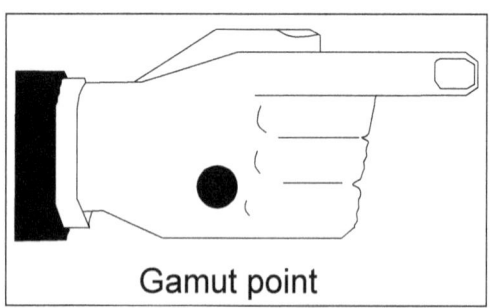
Gamut point

The Gamut Point is about 1/2 inch back from the space between your little finger and your ring finger. If you tap with 3 fingers you are sure to tap in the right spot.

An example of a residual issue affirmation might be:

"Even though there remains some residual feeling of negativity about (whatever was the initial issue)

I am willing to release this issue entirely

I am willing to release these things

I am willing to release the underlying emotional issues

I am willing to release the guilt that this represents and forgive myself and others and

I deeply, greatly and completely, love and approve of myself."

The procedure to clear any residue concerns:

1. **Whilst saying your statement about any residue of an issue, with your eyes closed**:-Tap the Gamut Point, only one spot, saying your affirmation all the way through. The affirmation needs to mention that this is about the residue of the initial issue. Breathe in and out as though you are letting go of the issue.

2. **Whilst saying your statement about any residue of an issue, with your eyes open**: Tap the Gamut Point, only one spot, saying your affirmation all the way through. The affirmation needs to mention that this is about the residue of the initial issue. At the end of the

tapping procedure, breathe in and out as though you are letting go of the issue.

3. **With your eyes open and looking down hard to the right (it may be uncomfortable)**: Tap the one spot whilst saying your statement. At the end of the tapping procedure, breathe in and out as though you are letting go of the issue.

4. **With your eyes open and looking down hard to the left (it may be uncomfortable)**: Tap the one spot whilst saying your statement. At the end of the tapping procedure, breathe in and out as though you are letting go of the issue.

5. **With your eyes open, roll your eyes all the way around in a circle in one direction**: Tap the one spot whilst saying your statement. At the end of the tapping procedure, breathe in and out as though you are letting go of the issue.

6. **In the reverse circle order, with your eyes open repeat your eye roll**: Tap the one spot whilst saying your statement. At the end of the tapping procedure, breathe in and out as though you are letting go of the issue.

7. **Hum 2- 5 seconds of a SONG, IT CAN BE ANY SONG whilst tapping (you will not be saying your statement in this step)**. At the end of the humming procedure, breathe in and out as though you are letting go of the issue.

8. **Count to five really quickly whilst tapping the one spot (you will not be saying your statement in this step.)** At the end of the counting procedure, breathe in and out as though you are letting go of the issue.

9. **Hum your song for 2 — 5 seconds whilst tapping the one spot (you will not be saying your statement during this step).** At the end of the humming procedure, breathe in and out as though you are letting go of the issue.

10. **Reassess the intensity of the residue of your emotion: to see where it lies on the Scale of 1 to 10.** If any residue remains repeat the normal tapping sequence first described. In the second run through of the tapping, you can skip the tapping on the hands and just do the head and body.

11. **If any residue still remains then do The Gamut Point tapping procedure once again.**

Gary Craig's Gamut Point Tapping Procedure can save you enormous amounts of time in ridding yourself of unwanted physical pain or emotional pain. The proof is in the doing. There are lots of videos available and literature and courses that you could do in order to be able to see what to do and how to do this. As I mentioned earlier, Andrew Lewis is an EFT Practitioner who can help you.

Summary of the general Tapping Procedure and The Gamut Procedure:

Tap through all of the points twice in the general tapping sequence. If there is only a slight reduction in relief of intensity of the issue then tap the Gamut Point. If there is still some residue then tap the body points again. You do not need to tap the points on the hands after having tapped once through the general procedure. Continue alternating between the usual procedure and The Gamut Point until relief is felt. Or, leave for another day and see what happens overnight.

1. **General Tapping Procedure**
2. **Use The Gamut Point Procedure**
3. **General Tapping Procedure - using the body points only (you do not have to include the points on the hands for the second or more times)**
4. **Repeat as necessary**

If I have used the procedures described above and there is still some residue of the issue remaining, I have found that this residue will disappear if I sleep on it. When I wake I generally feel that all is well and that the issue has been totally cleared.

EFT can be used for pretty much *anything*. I know that sounds an enormous claim! But EFT speaks for itself; once you have tried it, you'll see *how* you can use it for any issue you need to clear. EFT often works when *nothing else will*. The beauty is that you can do it *yourself*.

A final word of advice: Begin by using the General Procedure. If your issue is especially hard to release and it has not yet cleared, then move on to the Gamut Point Tapping Procedure to overcome *underlying beliefs*. Tapping can bypass *years* of therapy or analysing your past trying to get to those belief systems that hold you back. Quite often, you don't *need to know* what the underlying issue *is* that is holding you back. Using EFT, you can release deeply buried feelings of shame, resentment, and anger. You *will* feel emotional pain and physical pain *dissolve* in time. The beauty of EFT is that is works—even if you don't believe it will!

When you develop a daily practice of tapping to release trapped negativity, you will *see* how much room for forgiveness opens up within you. Ultimately, creating space for this forgiveness is the best thing you can do for yourself. Forgiveness *releases you to move on with your life*. It does not mean that you need to spend time with the person whom you needed to forgive—it simply means that you have empowered yourself by *taking the negative emotion out of your life*. It means that you can look at the person or the situation that was causing you pain and not feel the negative charge anymore. Forgiveness is liberating—it gives you back the freedom to choose what you want to do.

You see, *holding onto* a grudge, or maintaining the position of victim, or insisting, "I am right and you are wrong" only traps the rage within *you*. It's a lose-lose situation. Tragically, people often waste their whole lives holding onto this kind of negativity. Entire nations hold grudges for centuries. Imagine what life would be like if all that negative energy were cleared! It would reveal the truth underneath—that we are *meant* to be in a state of peace and harmony. Happiness and joy is our *natural* state. Imagine the power of coming from this miraculous place! All we need is a little change of perception—and a little willingness to forgive. The EFT procedure is a safe and reliable way to access the abundance of forgiveness that lies within you. It will help you find your way *back*—back to love.

10

Turbo Charge Getting What you Want (Daily Techniques)

"If you desire a different future, you must now have different thoughts and beliefs."

— **Raymond Aaron**

Step 5: Keeping your house in order; Part III: the Theta Mind

In Chapter 2, I mentioned a concept called the "theta mind." During the period of success when I was working on my movie—and regularly using the techniques I had learned in my Higher Consciousness Course—I was operating from the theta mind the entire time. This meant that things came easily and effortlessly. The objective of daily clearing—or cleansing of the aura and the chakras—is to allow connection with the Higher Self. Once this happens, you have *direct access* to all manner of resources to help you achieve the rich and meaningful life that you deserve.

Because I was in theta throughout the process of making my movie, all I had to do was set my goal and write it down. It was then a *foregone conclusion* that I would achieve it. I know that may sound incredible! But that is exactly what happened.

Staying in theta *maintained* my connection with my Higher Self; it kept me in a place of *knowingness*—the absolute certainty that I would succeed.

Now, I can hear you saying: I don't have the time to do a course for two years! And that's the way it is in today's society; when we want something, we want it now! Now, I understand this. I really do. And that is why I asked the universe to send me a technique that would *speed up* the process of getting into the theta mind.

Guess what? The universe did exactly that. I came across this wonderful technique by Asara Lovejoy called The One Command. This technique *incorporates* most of what I learned in the Higher Consciousness Course into a short, simplified form. It is a highly effective shortcut to goal setting and achievement. You may even see results *instantly*.

Coming from my natural talents base, as described by the Kolbe A Index in Chapter 5, I naturally decided to *simplify* Lovejoy's technique for my readers—so that you can use this technique quickly and effectively. The integrity of the process remains intact. I have simply added *clearer visuals* to aid your imagination, as well as the use of colours. These additions will clarify for you exactly what is happening at each stage of the process.

I have also included more detail about how to *refine your goals* for better outcomes. The other addition I have made to the information I came across in Lovejoy's book is a description of *how it feels to be in theta mind*.

It is also important to note that if you are not achieving a particular goal, you need to *repeat the goal* quite often and *focus* on the goal. You may also need to *restate* the goal in a different form. This can help to release the *underlying beliefs* that may be sabotaging your success. While these extra processes may add slightly to the time it takes to do The One Command, the benefits far outweigh the disadvantages.

Ultimately, the objective is to practise getting into theta mind as often as possible. This way, when you think of something you want—it comes *instantly*, whether you command it through the process or not. I know from experience, it really can get to the point where all you have to do is *think* of something with focus and clarity—and it appears. If you practice going into the theta mind daily, you will come to this place very quickly.

Just the other day, I was thinking about a particular goal that had not been reached yet. After giving it a bit of focus, I forgot about the goal completely and went about my day. Almost immediately, I got a phone call offering me *exactly* what I had stated in my initial command. You never know exactly when this kind of thing will happen, when what you want will appear. You don't have to know. You just need to *know that it will appear* in some form if you are persistent.

What is unusual about "The One Command," is that you only have to make a command once to be effective. It is true that you may not see the physical manifestation immediately — and some do in moments - but this is not an affirmation. It is rather an immediate rearrangement of your brain, biology and DNA. Lovejoy says that yes indeed you must make more commands. Here is what you need to know - every time you choose a positive path your negative limited thoughts will rise to meet you. After all they have been around a long time and don't understand yet, that there is a new way - a better way to live. As the next negative thought rises to the surface to oppose your success, that is your next command. Ask what you want instead and form your command from that desire. Lovejoy goes on to say this is, "Meeting yourself in the moment" to continue clearing your limiting ideas and beliefs. This is especially true if your DNA is heavily programmed in failure and self-sabotage. Be patient with yourself. Keep meeting yourself with the next negative occurrence to go forward toward your goal. And realize that you are getting into the practice of living the life you deserve! It is a practice to accept success.

The One Command system is based on the idea that if you can access your theta mind, you will have access to *untold resources and abundance*. These are the kinds of resources not readily available to us in our waking state or our beta state. In our beta state of mind, we constantly hook into things from the past and project things into the future. The beta state of mind is essentially a fearful state, as we are consumed with our past failures and our dread of failing again. How painful! And how unproductive!

Now, remember from Chapter 3 that we all have an underlying *sense of separation* from God, from our inner essence—our *natural* state of abundance and joy. The deep-seated awareness of this separation creates *guilt*, which we carry around with us all the time. This is the true source of our anxiety and fear. It is deeply rooted in the subconscious, whether we are fully aware of it or not.

The normal daily beta brainwave pattern that we use is very busy and results in the busy, cluttered thoughts that we continually have. Here's the important thing: The beta brainwave is our access to the past and the future. But it is only in the *present* that we can *enjoy the moment*; only by *being present* can we truly experience joy.

The problem is, of course, most of us *struggle* to get to the present! It is not easy. But only in the present can we experience the theta mind—the quiet, peaceful state in which we access our *rightful* abundance. Interestingly, these theta brainwaves are the ones we use when we are sleeping. In sleep we can access our limitless state, unhindered by negative thoughts, and we can draw abundance to us easily and effortlessly. So the objective is to get to the state that we experience when we are asleep, but to do so consciously, when we are awake.

Asara Lovejoy states: "In theta you connect to your natural, creative intelligence, and disengage from the fearful, limited worldview of what is possible. You develop a natural sense of security and trust in the world. The thoughts you have while in theta are more powerful than your ordinary thoughts, and they bring about changes in your life quickly and easily."

I am not going to go into the theoretical foundations of theta mind and all of the scientific background here, but needless to say, this body of work has been scientifically tested. Bruce Lipton's *The Biology of Belief* is an excellent book on the subject. Lipton's work provides valuable support for the idea that feelings of failure can be inherited through your DNA, as well as the existence of other dimensions and realities known to scientists, but of which the general population is unaware.

However, my job in this chapter is to give you the details of The One Command technique so that you can *shortcut* your way to those goals you made in Chapter 6. Remember to continue writing your goals for specific time periods such as 3 months, 6 months, a year, etc. The achievement of big life goals requires taking *one step at a time*, as each of your steps builds upon the last. I will now outline a detailed process of getting into theta mind with the One Command technique. After that I will then put it into summary form for ease of use. I will be using part of the previous techniques as outlined in Chapter 8, to get you grounded and focused.

The basic idea is to clear yourself first, become grounded and have access to the nurturing support of mother Earth, align with the command and your goal. Then, zoom up to the edges of the universe, and pop up through the clouds to that theta state.

Feel what it's like to be in theta, say your command, expand your thoughts and feelings, feel great gratitude, come back to earth, then accept the goal as received and that it will happen! Voila! Sounds easy, BUT it takes practice to flow smoothly, and as I said if your goal is not appearing, then you need to say it more frequently, restate it in another form or do some goals around limiting or conflicting beliefs first.

Along the way we will be using colours to heighten the experience and expanded feelings to lock in that success of achieving and receiving your desires. As I said earlier, I have added colour and heightened senses of experiencing your feelings.

The One Command Steps in detail:

1. **In a sitting position** (which could be in bed), close your eyes and take your giant imaginary pair of scissors and cut all ties to the past and future.
2. **Wash through with white light** using light spinning/circling through your body like a tornado to clear out the residue of negative thoughts. Wash through three

times and collect the gunk in your bag or balloon at your feet. Tie off the bag/balloon and release it out to the universe so that all the negativity disintegrates.

3. **Then sink your legs up to your mid-calf into the soft brown nurturing warmth of the earth.** As you are doing this, say to yourself something like this: "I am tapping into all of the love, nurturing, support and abundance the Earth offers me. I can feel the diamonds, rubies, sapphires, gold, silver, and pearls underneath my feet. I can feel abundance, or all the money I ever need is raining all over me."

In this step, we are trying to get you to feel that there is abundance available to you and all the love and nurture and support that you would ever need. So when your feet are in the earth and feeling that warmth breathe in and feel the abundance seeping through your body. Feel that everything that you ever need or ever want is available to you.

> As you breathe in with your feet firmly planted in the earth bring the feeling of the warmth of the earth up through your legs to the top of the legs and use the colour brown. The colour brown indicates strong support from the earth and that you feel deeply and firmly attached to the earth and all the support that you need. You will feel grounded.
>
> Breathe in the colour pink from the top of your legs right up your body to the top of your head. The colour pink indicates unconditional love, nurturing, and support from the earth. While still in this step have the colour pink fill your heart and expand and burst out from your heart spreading

right over all of the earth and its inhabitants. The colour goes right round the earth, encircling it and all of its inhabitants. It then comes right back through your back. As you are doing this feel the love and abundance for all persons and things on the earth wishing them all of the abundance you wish for yourself.

So the first three steps are helping you become **grounded** in getting you in the right frame of mind to ask the universe for your goal.

4. In this step you **repeat your command or state your goal** at the beta level with your eyes open, if you need to read it and to clarify, what it is. You are affirming that this is what you want clearly and precisely.

5. The next step is to **roll your eyes back in your head** looking behind the top of your eyebrows and trying to look up to the middle of the top of your head. This may be a little uncomfortable as it is not your usual position for your eyes. However, after a little practice it should become easier. The process of rolling your eyes back in your head looking to the top of your eyebrows or out of the top of your head is to get you into the theta state.

   Once you are in theta state and ready, the next part is to blast off into the outer reaches of the universe at lightning speed. Going to the edges of the universe gets us to theta, or the state of blissful awareness, that seems to be some place far away from your normal state of mind. The imagery is one of taking a journey to a wonderful place whereby we can ask for help.

How I blast off is, mentally I crouch down and I'm looking out through the top of my head and following this imaginary line, my flight path and then I push off rapidly to give me that boost that I need like a rocket going into outer space. Halfway through my journey I give myself another turbo blast to kick myself along the flight path and then the third time my turbo blast pops me up through the clouds and I land on a floating bed of clouds.

6. **Landing on a bed of clouds** gives you an imaginary, visual and a feeling of what theta might be like. Theta is a place where you feel like you are floating effortlessly, everything is easy and there are no limits. It is a place of total peace, bliss, and abundance. It is a place free of stress and tension and negativity.

My suggestion would be to take some time here in this lovely space to feel what theta is like and to experience the joy and the bliss. It is a place of total freedom. There are no restrictions or limitations. So enjoy that space before you get ready to say your command or your goal. Remember that your eyes are still looking up towards the top of your head/or the top of your eyebrows so that you can maintain the theta state. Feel the freedom. This is the place of abundance. This is the place of your natural birthright, a place of total connection to your higher self, a place where all the abundance you might ever want awaits for the asking.

7. Having experienced the bliss of theta you are now ready to **state your goal/command**, that your goal arrive from the Universe. In the book: The One Command, Asara Lovejoy states a formula for her command, which is as follows:

"I don't know how

> *I have .... (write out your goal in a very simple format)*
> *I only know that I do now, and*
> *I am fulfilled."*

Remember to keep your eyes rolled back, trying to look at the top of your head or the top of your eyebrows the whole time to maintain the theta state.

> Once I have said my goal, my command, I say to myself: "just let go", and I can feel all the tension and stress release from my body, my shoulders, the stress and any tension release and go right down through my legs and out to the bottom of my feet. Then I have my balloon or my bag ready to catch the gunk once again. I repeat my goal, state the command, and do the release process three times. Then I tie off the balloon or the bag and let it float off into the universe and disintegrate.

8. This step entails you feeling like **you have received your goal** or the information you need to receive it and at the same time you are changing your cells and your DNA to take account of these new changes in your life.

   So place yourself in a giant bubble. The colour green floods in as the new information you need, right through the top of your head. Breathe in and out. Then sprinkle gold dust within your balloon and feel gold dust tingling throughout your body. Your cells and your DNA vibrate with success and abundance. It is as though you're changing your DNA immediately. While this is happening, you are feeling the love, feeling the gratitude that all of these things are happening for you now rapidly, instantly. To help yourself along you can be saying: "Yes". "Thank you. Thank you. Thank you." You get excited at the prospect of success. Feel the feelings of success.

Within this step, your bubble is filled with green colour. Make the green colour go into your heart and expand your heart even further. It is as though your bubble expands much larger than before. At this stage, you feel as if you have achieved the goal that you have just stated. You now imagine what it would be like to achieve a much larger goal, something unexpected, an expanded version of your initial goal. This is the notion of expansion.

You are expanding from one idea to a much larger idea that you might achieve once you achieve your initial goal. You might expand into a notion of contributing to the planet or leaving a legacy for others to follow. The idea is to feel an idea much larger than your original goal in that state and when you do, your smaller goal will seem easier to achieve.

The objective whilst you are in theta is to imagine/feel or sense things happening to you. Feel feelings of success, great joy, gratitude and of expansion. Using colour therapy can help you achieve that more easily.

9. Once you feel you are ready to **come back down to earth**, simply roll your eyes back to the normal position and quietly slip back to earth. Once you are back on earth, take a giant imaginary rubber suction hose or vacuum cleaner and suck out from your body, all of the

residue negativity surrounding any thoughts you may have of not achieving your goal.

Suck out the negativity out of your head and out of your back and out of your lower back and out the bottom of your feet. Then make that vacuum cleaner or rubber suction hose disappear into the universe and disintegrate.

Then place yourself in a giant bubble and see the green colour pouring in through the top of your head all the information and resources that you need to achieve this goal here on earth. Then feel the sprinkles of gold dust. All through your body, in your head, in your arms, in your body and your legs and feel your cells and your DNA changing. Mentally, get up, and dance and say: "Yes. Thank you. Thank you. Thank you. Yes. I have achieved my goal. I have achieved my goal." So feel excited that this is going to happen and that it has happened already. So that is the process.

In summary, there are three stages:

1. **Preparation at ground level.**
2. **Travel through space and pop through the clouds to theta and issue your instruction, feel the changes and feel the gratitude.**
3. **Pop back to earth and accept consciously that you have achieved that goal.**

At each level we are using colours, words and feelings to really experience the process. The more that you can get your senses involved at all stages the greater experience you will have. I have found it useful just to practise going into theta mind several times a day without having any specific command or goal in mind. It is just to experience that peace and serenity, that bliss. How I do that is by simply rolling my eyes back to try to look out of the top of my head. I then feel that I am floating on clouds. I practise feeling the feelings of freedom, bliss and abundance. It is a habit that speeds up the achievement of my goals.

You might ask: what happens if I'm not achieving my goals and my commands aren't happening?

Remember earlier I said that people are equally afraid of failure and success, and because of this you may have limiting beliefs holding you back. In this situation, I would suggest you do the following and write an unedited version of what your life was like and your environment that you grew up with so you can see some of the patterns emerging in your life that you keep repeating.

I will give you an example:

My version of my early environment: when I was growing up I felt no support, nurture or love. There was no encouragement, direction, or strong role models in my life and I constantly felt that I did not belong, felt isolated and totally separate from, and independent from others. I did not trust others easily and felt that I could not rely on anyone and tended to do things by myself.

Okay, so from that you can see some basic beliefs that may have come back to haunt me throughout my life. Just choose one at a time to work on. So, the new command and goal that I needed to work on might be:

"I don't know how
I feel totally loved and supported in every situation
I only know I am now, and
I am fulfilled."

Another example could be:

"I don't know how
I am totally focused and maintaining direction in my life
I only know I am now, and
I am fulfilled."

Or another example might be:

"I don't know how
I release all resistance to receiving abundance in my life
I only know that I do now, and
I am fulfilled."

Grammatically some of these statements are incorrect. I believe that is to bypass the conscious mind to get to the subconscious mind. If you give the conscious mind a task it gets busy doing that and leaves the real process to the part of the mind that you really want to reach.

So, if you are not achieving your goals keep looking at your environmental examples to clear up limiting beliefs or keep tweaking your goal until it comes true. This may take some time. However, the benefits are truly worth it.

Sometimes the results can be instant, sometimes results are sent as thoughts which outline the steps you need to take or the right people will show up to deliver some aspect of your goal. Be open to receiving and life will bring its magic.

So just to outline a summary of the process (as per The One Command book):

1. The first step is to **ground** yourself - (white light cleanse/brown legs/pink body, feel the feelings)
2. **Align** yourself to you goal - say your goal to yourself before zooming off into space - (pink circle around the earth)
3. Get to **theta** - the clouds - (feel the abundance and limitlessness)
4. Do your **commands**/your goals three times- let go (tie off the gunk into your balloon or bag)
5. **Expand the feeling**- (green colour, sprinkle gold, feel the feelings)
6. **Receive** with gratitude in theta- say: thank you, thank you, thank you and come back to earth and receive with gratitude in beta- (green colour, sprinkle gold, feel the feelings)

Using the simplified One Command technique, you can invite greater opportunities for joy and peace into your life. You will find over time that your perspective will change on a fundamental level; you will feel lighter and more joyful. Even if that were all you achieved in this lifetime, you would be better off than 85% of the rest of the planet!

If, instead, you carry around feelings of resentment, bitterness, or anger, then you truly *can't attract* the abundance that you deserve. I can say this with authority because it has happened to me. And yes, success is a process—an *ongoing process*. It requires a bit of maintenance, even as it opens up exciting new possibilities each day! So, I encourage you to incorporate these daily techniques into your life—and be open to the abundance and the beauty they *will* bring to you. (Please see the Permissions and Resources Page for more information.)

11

Putting it All Together — A Blueprint for Success

"We are what we repeatedly do; excellence, then, is not an act but a habit."

— **Aristotle**

Now that we've looked at each of the five steps in detail, let's put them all together. This chapter is a summary of the steps and how I moved through them personally. Let this be your shortcut to living the life you deserve, now!

For years I didn't have a spiritual home. I didn't feel that I belonged anywhere. Being brought up in a Catholic environment, I always felt the wrath of a vengeful God. I also witnessed so many terrible examples of non-Christian behaviour in that environment! It's no wonder that religion was all over for me the moment I left the iron gates of my Catholic school behind me.

I didn't have a strong sense of belonging growing up. I always felt that I was different from my parents and siblings. I had a different attitude, different beliefs. So, essentially when I left high school I wandered off alone into the world. I was looking for something, something that was missing. I tried to find it in marriage, but I now see that at that time I did not have the necessary skills to create a lasting, life-long relationship.

I tried to find it in working, friends, parties, courses, degrees... and so on. I stumbled into the personal development arena in my searches and I really couldn't have been any more motivated if I tried. However, nothing lasted; it didn't stick, didn't make sense. Nothing really answered the question of what was missing.

I was engulfed in a void of alienation, isolation. I had a profound sense of *separation*. I had no direction and I felt deeply hopeless—even though none of this was evident from the outside. For all appearances, I looked like I was holding it together pretty well.

Then I came across the Higher Consciousness Course and, finally, I had a sense of belonging. Finally, I was connecting with spirit and my true essence. Operating from that space I was able to create, to manifest out of nothing but a few words on a page! The result was that over 120 people came on board and helped me make my movie.

Making the movie connected me with a feeling of limitless abundance. Without even realising it, I was at that time acting out the steps to living the life I deserved. On that path, I saw clearly what my greatest gifts were: creativity, intuition, and inspiration. These are my highest value qualities, and on the right path I excelled in all of them. I now understand that this is where I need to concentrate my future efforts. Unfortunately, I didn't know it at the time. There was still something missing.

When I completed the Higher Consciousness Course and left the group, something happened that I had not predicted.

My support network—both internal and external—gradually disappeared. I found myself wandering aimlessly from job to job, group to group—trying to recapture that missing link. I wasn't even sure what the missing link was. I only knew I didn't have it. I didn't feel that I belonged here, there or anywhere in particular. I felt that I'd been dumped on another planet and they weren't coming back to get me.

From this experience, I have come to realise that the *environment that you place yourself in must be one that deliberately nurtures and supports you.* Your environment must support the individual you truly are; it must recognise and validate your identity. All too often, we drastically underestimate the influence of environment. Being in the wrong environment can make us feel alienated, self-doubting, unsure of our gifts and skills. All of these feelings equal *lack of love.* I know this from what happened after I made my movie. Even if you follow all of the five steps I've outlined and you are motivated beyond belief—it will come to nothing if your environment is not supportive. The best work and the best intentions cannot survive if there is an overall lack of love. Bad habits pull you back to your former ways.

When I graduated from the Higher Consciousness Course I joined another group and felt that I had a life path. At least, I still had a sense of my earthly purpose and direction. But this really wasn't enough, because this new group lacked the important element of spirituality. I felt this absence deeply, even though I couldn't exactly identify it. You see, even if you *are* on a productive life path, and you are contributing meaningfully to the world around you—it will not last if there is no spiritual connection. This aspect—this connection with your *true self*— is the foundation that you need for *lasting* success.

I came upon it in A Course in Miracles. Finally, I had an answer for why I had such a deep sense of not belonging, of feeling separate not only from everyone on the planet, but also from my essence, my true self.

A Course in Miracles gave me my blueprint. Through it, I learnt my *spiritual purpose*. The principle of the original separation outlined in *ACIM* explained perfectly how the ego mind keeps us in a place of fear, judgment, and self-doubt. I began to see how—in the absence of a connection with our real spiritual purpose—we are living with a profound *lack of love*. This was such a revelation! At last, I understood my perpetual sense of *not belonging*. Finally, I began so see where I did belong.

I learnt to see others as part of a greater whole inclusive of *everything*—myself, the world, God/the Source. I saw the *real truth* that if you attack another, you attack yourself. You attack God. The true essence of each of us is Godlike; so, when I say "God" I am also talking about "Self." When I discovered the divine in the universe, God/the Source — I discovered myself. To stay in communication with this divinity that resides in me, I must maintain a connection with my Higher Self. This connection, this daily fine-tuning of my intuitive skills, is the basis of all happiness and success.

We each have this ability—the inner voice that gives us flashes of insight. This is the part of us that can override the beta mind. So often, though, feelings of failure and lack drown out the true message of love and support that your Higher Self can give you. The *key* to keeping the real message coming through—the message of *love and abundance* — is forgiveness. I don't believe you can be truly able to attract what you deserve in this life unless you come from the position of *forgiveness*. This is the basis of all love, love for yourself and love for others. Forgiveness frees you of the negative energy that ties you to another. It frees both of you. Forgiveness allows you to achieve greater heights of happiness and success. It connects us all to the same source, the place where we are all one, where we overcome our deep and painful sense of separation—and we reconnect with spirit, with love.

Through these principles, I have found my structure for living the life I deserve. I have a foundation of my spiritual purpose, upon which I have built a framework to live. I know why I am here. *I am here to forgive.* To forgive myself for accepting the ego's plan for self-destruction and to forgive others so they are free to do the same.

Finding my spiritual purpose gave me the rock, the home that I needed. That was Step 1. Then, I discovered the Wealth Dynamics Profiling System—the formal system I needed to help me define my Life Path. This is Step 2: Getting on your correct Life Path, clarifying your identity, and finding your life purpose/s. To do this, you must discover your set of natural talents that you were born with. This allows you to focus on your true career, your true life purpose.

The Wealth Dynamics Profiling System pointed me in the direction of the Star Profile, with a strong backup in the Creator Profile. This made me see that so many of those little things I do naturally— so naturally I don't even think of them as skills— *are* skills. They are my real, natural talents. Understanding this also showed me *the environment* that I need to be in, in order to achieve the success that I want.

If I follow my Star Profile, I *will* create my greatest wealth. And by wealth I mean both inner *and* outer wealth. Within the Star Profile, I need to refine and fine-tune my brand constantly.

I am meant to lead from the front, inspiring and motivating people. I must be a role model and all that entails. In my business I am my own product. My brand is my personality. If I am using my particular natural talents, I will welcome the greatest possible abundance into my life.

Everyone has natural talents. I urge you to discover yours. Sometimes they are hidden from you because you've become so used to using learned skills instead. These types of skills are generally the ones you learn when you pursue a specific career, e.g. becoming an accountant, a lawyer, a doctor and so on. Learned skills can keep us trapped on the wrong life path if we don't look inside and figure out our real natural talents base. It takes courage to do this, but I promise you it feels so liberating to have your natural skills acknowledged. Your efforts actually become easier because you are working from a *natural* place!

Once you've identified your general profile, you will want to fine-tune what specific natural talents you have so that you can use them to your best advantage. During my Step 2, I took the Kolbe A Index, which is so *personalised* that only 5% of the population is likely to share my results. The Kolbe A Index showed that I was an *Innovator*. I should spend 56% of my time and energy in the Quick Start Mode, taking on high-potential challenges. In this mode, I am utilising my greatest potential.

Using this information, I can see that *any* job, career, or business that I undertake must incorporate the following:

- The freedom to experiment and take significant risks
- The potential to challenge myself with deadlines and tough-to-reach goals

- Frequent interruptions that bring diversity and provide brainstorming opportunities.

If these things are at play in my life, I will feel nurtured for my strengths and free to be myself! Apparently I am terrific with future-oriented challenges and dealing with the essential facts. If I have more information than I need, it becomes overwhelming and I need to *simplify*.

So, with my Life Path identified and my true natural talents clarified I am now ready to define my life mission, my human life purpose. I have my *true identity*. This is a wonderfully validating and liberating feeling. Understanding clearly my strengths and weaknesses shows me what I need to do to create a fulfilling life.

Path + Clarity of natural talents base = Identity, which leads to Purpose. So, within My Star Profile from the Wealth Dynamics Profiling System, together with the clarity I have around my natural talents base from the Kolbe A Index, I have great clarity around my identity. From this path, I have now identified three human life purposes or life missions. These include work, spiritual and personal purposes:

- to be an inspirational teacher
- to make a contribution on the planet
- to have magical relationships.

With these elements in place, I can move onto Step 3: creating meaningful goals. These goals will get me to the place I *know* I "should" be going rather than a place everyone else says I "should" be. Knowing my *true self*, my true natural talents, I can choose business, job and career endeavours that create the greatest amount of wealth for me, including personal/spiritual *as well as* financial wealth. I now have *permission to be myself.* It is a place of true validation. Knowing who I am, knowing that my particular skill set is useable and feeling valued for it—this is the most liberating feeling you can imagine! Furthermore, my path to success is always supported by my strong connection with my Higher Self. Maintaining this connection will keep you on the fast track to success. In fact, I do not believe that success can truly be fulfilling and lasting without it.

So, once you have identified your Life Path and acknowledged your true natural talents, clarified your identity and outlined your purposes, I urge you to write out your long-term goals. Your goals will now revolve around your stated life purposes. These may change over time or you may refine your direction. Break these long-term goals into yearly goals and three-monthly goals. This process will ultimately lead you to work out what needs to be done monthly, weekly, and daily. Writing out your goals will help you keep focused and give you direction, clarity and a sense of purpose. Also, you're more likely to achieve your goals if they are written down.

Throughout your journey, you need to be mindful of the power of the tool of forgiveness, Step 4. Forgive yourself for being too hard on yourself or impatient for things to happen. Forgive others for what appears to be interference or *wrong* opinions. When you get angry step back and examine what is happening in that moment. Remember the umbrella of love, for yourself and others.

In Step 5, I outlined several easy techniques to help you keep focused and clear yourself of the doubts and fears that the ego mind constantly throws up at you to keep you off track. And boy does that work! The ego mind is, unfortunately, very good at its job. That's why my goal for you is to make the *theta mind* your overriding state for all of your decisions. It truly is a place of inner peace and bliss. To help you stay in on track, you can use the White Light Cleansing and the Daily Intention each day. The Sea of Abundance keeps you topped up throughout the day. Using Guided Meditation as well can hone your senses, your intuition, and your imagination. Using EFT rids your body of old emotional issues and negative beliefs, making it easier to allow forgiveness into your life for those situations that call for it.

And finally, we learnt The One Command technique, to help us get into the theta mind and achieve our goals more easily and effortlessly. This is a place where we connect with our true essence, our Higher Self/the Holy Spirit. This is the *source mind*, a place where we are all joined as one. It is the place of limitless abundance, of inner peace, joy, freedom, and fulfilment. When you are operating from this place, abundance comes to you effortlessly.

I used the story of my film as an example of the five-step process. This helped me to identify the steps and to remember what it felt like to be in flow. Now that I have examined more deeply the keys to real and lasting success, I am able to replicate these steps easily and effortlessly on a daily basis. I invite you to join with me to do the same! (Please see my Invitation at the end of this book).

You see, it is the ego mind—which can also be called the beta mind—that creates negativity and keeps us in a place of fear and failure. But this is not the *true reality*! Rather, it is the theta mind that is our birthright. This is the state of limitless love, achievement, and inner peace that is our *natural state*. When we find our way back to this place, we can stay connected with our Higher Self, our God-like self. From here, resources appear effortlessly and abundance flows.

I do hope that I have shown you how truly easy this can be! It's really about taking action, taking baby steps. I know from experience that you can go to seminar after seminar, meet guru after guru and, ultimately, you will notice that it's all leading to the same place. All the self-development literature, at its core, is heading towards *heart*, but they leave out the key tool of forgiveness! Without this, you will only be attempting to follow someone else's path or prescription. My goal is for you to find *your own true path*.

Here are the 5 Steps once more. In order to find *your* Path, to clearly define yourself and start living the life you deserve, NOW—not sometime in the future:

1. **Identify your foundation**. This is your *spiritual life purpose*. Discovering this, you will have a home, a rock solid foundation from which to operate. A spiritual foundation gives you clearly defined values and belief systems. These may change over time, but it's important to have a base from which to start. This forms your inner support system for the rest of your life. You will gain an understanding of where you fit and how to overcome our only real problem on this planet—our separation from God, from our true essence of love, our separation from ourselves. Re-connecting with your inner self—with love—is the key to your spiritual foundation.

2. **Find your framework**. This means finding your Life Path, finding clarity around your identity and defining

your life purposes. To do this, you need to clarify who you really are and what your unique natural talents are to deliver your promise to the planet. Remember that your life purpose may be different from other people's. For example, you might want to be a great accountant, you might want to be a great parent, or you might want to be a great brother or sister. *Every life purpose is meaningful* whether it is great or small. Everybody has a human job to do while they are here, apart from the overriding job of loving yourself and others.

3. **Build your fence**. Once you have identified your spiritual foundation, your human Life Path, clarified your identity and defined your natural talents base, and discovered your life purposes, you are ready to set meaningful goals. And *write them down*. Set your yearly goal/s at the end of the year *as though you have already achieved them*. Then work backwards, breaking your goals up on a three- monthly, monthly, weekly, or daily basis. These could be as simple as "to-do" lists. Remember, baby steps are fine! The key is taking some kind of step every day—whether it's just a deed, a word or a thought toward your overall plan. (If you are a detail-oriented person, you will want to break your goals down very specifically. See Raymond Aaron's Double Your Income website in the Resources Page for templates to assist with this.)

4. **Use the key of forgiveness**. The umbrella of love requires forgiveness to keep you on track, protected and nurtured in all your efforts. You can rid yourself of negativity in any situation through forgiveness, freeing up your energy for more productive uses! You do this by remembering

that anger or attacks directed at someone else are actually attacks against *your own God-like self*. Forgiveness is the ultimate tool that draws the attractiveness factor into your life. Maintaining resentment, bitterness, anger, fear or a sense of lack in any area of your life effectively *blocks* abundance from speeding towards you. Lack blocks abundance; love *invites* it.

5. **Keep your house in order**. Use simple daily techniques to stay on track. Stay positive and open with chakra colour therapy. Clear your aura with the White Light Wash. Practice Daily Intention, Sea of Abundance and Guided Meditation to keep yourself free of negativity. Practice forgiveness daily with physical and conscious level techniques such as tapping for EFT. To turbocharge your goal achievement at the theta level, incorporate The One Command technique with colour therapy. Remember, *success breeds success*. Forming daily success habits will keep the abundance flowing!

In short, these are the **five steps to living the life you deserve, now**! I invite you to join me on the journey (see the Special Invitation for you at the end of this book). Discover and clarify your true identity, at all levels. I invite you to meet your *true self*, your essence and, through this introduction, to discover your own unique Path to joy, healing, happiness, passion, success and abundance in all areas of your life — *NOW!*

I am just so excited to be able to share this information with you and I look forward to meeting you all personally very soon.

I hope you have enjoyed reading my book and perhaps you will take this opportunity to change your life. I encourage you to take the first step towards loving yourself: finding out who you *really* are, why you are here and what the Right Path is for you. You cannot possibly imagine how liberating this feeling is. It's as though someone really "gets you." You will feel validated, excited about starting your life afresh! You will re-connect to your passions; however hidden they may be at present.

True happiness, inner peace, joy, abundance, deep passion and lasting success in your work, your career, and your life spring from loving yourself and others. These five steps are a blueprint for a way back to love. There is only one common spiritual *and* human life purpose—and actually, it's about love!

From the Heart
Trish Mackenzie
www.learntobesuccessfulnow.com

To obtain your **FREE Bonuses** mentioned throughout the book please go to

www.learntobesuccessfulnow.com

and enter the **VIP Code: AAL51** or your **Order Number**.

Permissions and Resources Page

Permissions

Raymond Aaron, www.doubleyourincomedoingwhatyoulove.com

Roger Hamilton, Wealth Dynamics Profile, www.resultsfoundation.com

David Kolbe, The Kolbe A™ Index, www.kolbe.com

Andrew Lewis, International EFT Trainer, For The Tapping Information and Diagrams, www.emofree.com.au

Information on The One Command is presented with the author, Asara Lovejoy's permission.

To learn more about the complete process go to get your free PDF of the Six Steps and The One Command video by Asara that takes you through the process at www.bookguide.asara.com and learn more at www.theonecommandlife.com.

Resources

Raymond Aaron, *www.aarongroup.com*

Raymond Aaron, *www.doubleyourincomedoingwhatyoulove.com*

Raymond Aaron, *www.visibilityancredibility.com*

Raymond Aaron, *www.OwnTheEdge.com*

Jeff Vacek and Ken Preuss, *www.inforenegades.com*

Paul Blackburn, *www.beyondsuccess.com.au*

Andrew Lewis, *www.emofree.com.au*

Roger James Hamilton, *www.resultsfoundation.com*

Roger James Hamilton, *www.wealthdynamics.com*

Kathy Kolbe, *www.kolbe.com*

Asara Lovejoy, *www.theonecommand.com*

JT Foxx, *www.jtfoxx.com*

Nina Sunday, *www.HowToStudyMethod.com.au*

www.nightingale-conant.com

Paul Scheele, *www.learningstrategies.com*

Neale Donald Walshe, *www.nealedonaldwalshe.com*

Stedman Graham, *www.stedmangraham.com*

Steven Bradbury, *Last Man Standing*

Bob Proctor, *Born Rich*

Anthony Robbins, *Creating Lasting Change*

Steven Covey, *The 7 Habits of Highly Effective People*

Napoleon Hill, *Think and Grow Rich*

Wayne Dyer, *How to be a No-Limit Person*

Louse Hay, *You Can Heal Your Life*

Mona-Lisa Schultz, *Awakening Intuition*

Marianne Williamson, *A Return to Love*, www.mariannewilliamson.com

Foundation for Inner Peace, *A Course in Miracles*

Jean Houston, *The Possible Human*

Jim Rohn, *The Seasons of Life*

Rick Ott, *Creating Demand*

John Gabriel, www.gabrielmethod.com

Doreen Virtue, *Angel Cards*

Byron Katie, *Loving What Is*

Rick Scheinfeld, *Busting Loose*

Joe Vitale, *The Attractor Factor*

Richard Branson, *Screw It, Just Do It!*

The Secret, DVD and Book

Dr Mark Hyman, *The Five Forces of Wellness*

Nightingale Learning Systems, *The FlexBrain Method*

Zig Ziglar, *A View From The Top*

A Thank You Card for Someone Special

Dear New Friend,

Thank you so much for buying my book and taking the time to read it.

I hope you have found something in these pages that encourages you to take direct action to change your life, to become the person you really are and to invite more passion, happiness and success into your career by uncovering your identity, and by reconnecting with your natural talents base. I hope you have found the way to your true Life Path and Life Purpose/s. Remember, it's about decision. It's about taking action.

If this message has resonated with you please tell your friends, knowing you will contribute to their overall happiness and Life Path and Life Purpose fulfillment. Thank you for sharing with your friends, your generosity and on-going support. Please visit:
www.learnto besuccessfulnow.com

From the Heart,

Trish Mackenzie

A Special Invitation

Attention Frustrated Working Women Who Want to Fast Track Their Career Success…

**Join Us on: The 7 Week E-Course:
Identity: The Key to Fast Track Your Career Success**

THE 5- Step Blueprint to Discovering Your Identity, Greater Self Love, Passion, Happiness and Success

What you will learn:

- understand your spiritual foundation
- how to reconnect with your inner essence
- discover your Life Path, and gain clarity around your natural talents base,
- reconnect with your passions and uncover your human life purpose/s
- discover and clarify your identity
- set meaningful goals around your new identity
- how to live with love and forgive and move on in any situation
- techniques to maintain and enhance your new life focus

**Visit the website and send an Email to Register your interest in attending this special
7 Week E Course Event at:**

www.learntobesuccessfulnow.com

I look forward to meeting you personally very soon.

From the Heart,

Trish Mackenzie

www.ingramcontent.com/pod-product-compliance
Lightning Source LLC
Chambersburg PA
CBHW060532100426
42743CB00009B/1505